YOUR PERSONAL
HOROSCOPE
2019

SAGITTARIUS

YOUR PERSONAL HOROSCOPE 2019

SAGITTARIUS

23rd November–21st December

igloobooks

Published in 2018
by Igloo Books Ltd
Cottage Farm
Sywell
NN6 0BJ
www.igloobooks.com

Produced for Igloo Books by Foulsham Publishing Ltd, The Old Barrel Store,
Drayman's Lane, Marlow, Bucks SL7 2FF, England

FIR003 0718
2 4 6 8 10 9 7 5 3 1
ISBN: 978-1-78810-539-2

This is an abridged version of material originally published
in Old Moore's Horoscope and Astral Diary.

Cover designed by Nicholas Gage
Edited by Bobby Newlyn-Jones

Printed and manufactured in China

CONTENTS

INTRODUCTION

Your personal horoscopes have been specifically created to allow you to get the most from astrological patterns and the way they have a bearing on not only your zodiac sign, but nuances within it. Using the diary section of the book you can read about the influences and possibilities of each and every day of the year. It will be possible for you to see when you are likely to be cheerful and happy or those times when your nature is in retreat and you will be more circumspect. The diary will help to give you a feel for the specific 'cycles' of astrology and the way they can subtly change your day-to-day life. For example, when you see the sign ☿, this means that the planet Mercury is retrograde at that time. Retrograde means it appears to be running backwards through the zodiac. Such a happening has a significant effect on communication skills, but this is only one small aspect of how the personal horoscope can help you.

With your personal horoscope the story doesn't end with the diary pages. It includes simple ways for you to work out the zodiac sign the Moon occupied at the time of your birth, and what this means for your personality. In addition, if you know the time of day you were born, it is possible to discover your Ascendant, yet another important guide to your personal make-up and potential.

Many readers are interested in relationships and in knowing how well they get on with people of other astrological signs. You might also be interested in the way you appear to very different sorts of individuals. If you are such a person, the section on Venus will be of particular interest. Despite the rapidly changing position of this planet, you can work out your Venus sign, and learn what bearing it will have on your life.

Using your personal horoscope you can travel on one of the most fascinating and rewarding journeys that anyone can take – the journey to a better realisation of self.

INTRODUCTION

THE ESSENCE OF SAGITTARIUS

Exploring the Personality of Sagittarius the Archer

(23RD NOVEMBER – 21ST DECEMBER)

What's in a sign?

Sagittarius is ruled by the large, expansive planet Jupiter, which from an astrological perspective makes all the difference to this happy-go-lucky and very enterprising zodiac sign. This is the sign of the Archer and there is a very good reason for our ancient ancestors having chosen the half-man, half-horse figure with its drawn bow. Not only are Sagittarians fleet-footed like a horse, but the remarks they make, like the arrow, go right to the target.

You love contentious situations and rarely shy away from controversy. With tremendous faith in your own abilities you are not easily kept down, and would usually find it relatively simple to persuade others to follow your course. Though you are born of a Fire sign, you are not as bullying as Aries can be, or as proud as a Leo. Despite this you do have a Fire-sign temper and can be a formidable opponent once you have your dander up.

You rarely choose to take the long route to any destination in life, preferring to drive forward as soon as your mind is made up. Communication comes easy to you and you add to your stock of weapons good intuitive insight and a capacity for brinkmanship that appears to know no bounds. At your best you are earnest, aspiring and honourable, though on the other side of the coin Sagittarians can make the best con artists of all!

What you hate most is to be discouraged, or for others to thwart your intentions. There is a slight tendency for you to use others whilst you are engaging in many of the schemes that are an intrinsic part of your life, though you would never deliberately hurt or offend anyone.

Sagittarian people are natural lovers of fun. When what is required is a shot of enthusiasm, or an immediacy that can cut right through the middle of any red tape, it is the Archer who invariably ends up in charge. When others panic, you come into your own, and you have an ability to get things done in a quarter of the expected time. Whether they are completed perfectly, however, is a different matter altogether.

Sagittarius resources

Sagittarians appear to be the natural conjurors of the zodiac. The stage magician seems to draw objects from thin air, and it often appears that the Archer is able to do something similar. This is an intriguing process to observe, but somewhat difficult to explain. Sagittarians seem to be able to get directly to the heart of any matter, and find it easy to circumnavigate potential difficulties. Thus they achieve objectives that look impossible to observers – hence the conjuring analogy.

Just as the biblical David managed to defeat Goliath with nothing more than a humble pebble and a sling, Sagittarius also goes seemingly naked into battle. The Archer relies on his or her natural wit, together with a fairly instinctive intelligence, a good deal of common sense and a silver tongue. The patient observer must inevitably come to the conclusion that what really matters isn't what the Sagittarian can do, but how much they manage to get others to undertake on their behalf. In other words, people follow your lead without question. This quality can be one of your best resources and only fails when you have doubts about yourself, which fortunately is very rarely.

If other signs could sell refrigerators to Eskimos, you could add a deep-freeze complete with ice tray! This is one of the reasons why so many Archers are engaged in both advertising and marketing. Not only do you know what people want, you also have an instinctive ability to make them want whatever it is you have on offer.

It is likely that you would see nothing remotely mysterious about your ability to peer through to the heart of any matter. In the main you would refer to this as 'gut reaction', despite the fact that it looks distinctly magical to those around you. Fortunately this is part of your mystique, and even if you should choose to take someone for a complete ride, it is doubtful that they would end up disliking you as a result. You don't set out to be considered a genius, and you manage to retain the common touch. This is extremely important, for those with whom you have contacts actively want to help you because you are a 'regular guy'.

Beneath the surface

People tend to be very complicated. Untangling their motives in any given situation is rarely easy. Psychologists have many theories regarding the working of the human psyche and philosophers have struggled with such matters for thousands of years. Clearly none of these people were looking at the zodiac sign of Sagittarius. Ask the average Archer why they did this or that thing and the chances are that you will get a reply something very similar to 'Well, it seemed like a good idea at the time'.

While many people might claim to be uncomplicated, at heart you genuinely are. Complications are something you try to avoid, even though some of your deals in life might look like a roll of barbed wire to those around you. In the main you keep your objectives as simple as possible. This is one of the reasons why it isn't particularly difficult for you to circumnavigate some of the potential pitfalls – you simply won't recognise that they exist. Setting your eyes on the horizon you set off with a jaunty step, refusing to acknowledge problems and, when necessary, sorting them out on the way.

Your general intention is to succeed and this fact permeates just about every facet of your life. Satisfaction doesn't necessarily come for you from a job well done, because the word 'well' in this context often isn't especially important. And when you have one task out of the way, you immediately set your sights on something else. Trying to figure out exactly why you live your life in the way you do, your psychological imperatives and ultimate intentions, costs you too much time, so you probably don't indulge in such idle speculation at all.

You have a warm heart and always want the best for everyone. It almost never occurs to you that other people don't think about things in the way you might and you automatically assume that others will be only too pleased to follow your lead. In the main you are uncomplicated, don't indulge in too many frills and fancies and speak your mind. There really isn't much difference between what you do in life, and what you think about your actions. This is not to infer that you are shallow, merely that you don't see much point in complicating the obvious with too much internal musing.

One of the main reasons why people like you so much is because the 'what you see is what you get' adage is more true in your case than in any other.

Making the best of yourself

Always on the go and invariably looking for a new challenge, it isn't hard to see how Sagittarius makes the best of itself. This is a dynamic, thrusting sign, with a thirst for adventure and a great ability to think on its feet. As a child of Sagittarius you need the cut and thrust of an exciting life in order to show your true mettle. It doesn't do for you to sit around inactive for any length of time and any sort of enforced lay-off is likely to drive you to distraction.

In a career situation your natural proclivities show through, so it's best for you to be in some position which necessitates decision making on a moment-by-moment basis. Production-line work or tasks that involve going over the same ground time and again are not really your forte, though you are certainly not afraid of hard work and can labour on regardless towards any objective – just as long as there is a degree of excitement on the way.

Socially speaking you probably have many friends, and that's the way you like things to be. You need to know that people rate you highly, and will usually be on hand to offer the sort of advice that is always interesting, but probably not totally reasoned. It's a fact that you think everyone has the same ability to think on their feet that typifies your nature, and you trust everyone instinctively – at least once.

In love you need the sort of relationship that allows a degree of personal freedom. You can't be fettered and so have to be your own person under all situations. You are kind and attentive, though sometimes get carried away with the next grand scheme and so you need an understanding partner. Archers should not tie themselves down too early in life and are at their best surrounded by those who love the dynamism and difficult-to-predict qualities exemplified by this zodiac sign.

Most important of all you need to be happy with your lot. Living through restricted or miserable times takes its toll. Fortunately these are few in your life, mainly because of the effort you put into life yourself.

The impressions you give

You must be doing something right because it's a fact that Sagittarius represents one of the most instinctively liked zodiac signs. There are many reasons for this state of affairs. For starters you will always do others a good turn if it's possible. It's true that you are a bit of a rogue on occasions, but that only endears you to the sort of individuals with whom you choose to share your life. You are always the first with a joke, even under difficult circumstances, and you face problems with an open mind and a determination to get through them. On the way you acquire many friends, though in your case many 'acquaintances' might be nearer the mark. This is a situation of your own choosing and though you have so much to recommend you to others, it's a fact that you keep really close ties to the absolute minimum.

Some people might think you rather superficial and perhaps an intellectual lightweight. If so, this only comes about because they don't understand the way your mind works. All the same it is your own nature that leads a few individuals to these conclusions. You can skip from one subject to another, are an insatiable flirt in social situations and love to tell funny stories. 'Depth' isn't really your thing and that means that you could appear to lower the tone of conversations that are getting too heavy for your liking. You do need to be the centre of attention most of the time, which won't exactly endear you to others who have a similar disposition.

People know that you have a temper, like all Fire signs. They will also realise that your outbursts are rare, short-lived and of no real note. You don't bear a grudge and quickly learn that friends are more useful than enemies under any circumstance.

You come across as the capricious, bubbly, lively, likeable child of the zodiac and under such circumstances it would be very difficult for anyone to find fault with you for long. Often outrageous, always interesting and seldom down in the dumps – it's hard to see how you could fail to be loved.

The way forward

It might be best to realise, right from the outset, that you are not indestructible. Deep inside you have all the same insecurities, vulnerabilities and paranoia that the rest of humanity possesses. As a Sagittarian it doesn't do to dwell on such matters, but at least the acknowledgement might stop you going over the edge sometimes. You come from a part of the zodiac that has to be active and which must show itself in the best possible light all the time, and that's a process that is very demanding.

In the main, however, you relish the cut and thrust of life and it is quite likely that you already have the necessary recipe for happiness and success. If you don't, then you are involved in a search that is likely to be both interesting and rewarding, because it isn't really the objective that matters to you but rather the fun you can have on the way.

Be as honest as you can with those around you, though without losing that slightly roguish charm that makes you so appealing. At the same time try to ensure that your own objectives bear others in mind. You can sometimes be a little fickle and, in rare circumstances, unscrupulous. At heart though, you have your own moral convictions and would rarely do anyone a bad turn. On the contrary, you do your best to help those around you, and invariably gain in popularity on the way.

Health-wise you are probably fairly robust but you can run your nervous system into the ground on occasions. There are times when a definite routine suits you physically, but this doesn't always agree with your mental make-up, which is essentially driving and demanding. The peaks and troughs of your life are an inevitable part of what makes you tick, and you would be a poorer person without them.

Explaining yourself is not generally difficult, and neither is the search for personal success, even if you keep looking beyond it to even greater achievements further down the road. Being loved is important, despite the fact that you would deny this on occasions. Perhaps you don't always know yourself as well as you might, though since you are not an inveterate deep thinker it is likely that this is not a problem to you.

If you are already an adult, it's likely the path you are presently following is the one for you. That doesn't mean to say that you will keep to it, or find it universally rewarding. You find new promise in each day, and that's the joy of Sagittarius.

SAGITTARIUS ON THE CUSP

Astrological profiles are altered for those people born at either the beginning or the end of a zodiac sign, or, more properly, on the cusps of a sign. In the case of Sagittarius this would be on the 23rd of November and for two or three days after, and similarly at the end of the sign, probably from the 19th to the 21st of December.

The Scorpio Cusp – 23rd November to 25th November

You could turn out to be one of the most well-liked people around, especially if you draw heavily from the more positive qualities of the two zodiac signs that have the most profound part to play in your life. Taken alone the Sagittarian is often accused of being rather too flighty. Sagittarians are often guilty of flirting and sometimes fall foul of people who take a more serious view of life in general. The presence in your make-up of the much deeper and more contemplative sign of Scorpio brings a quiet and a sense of reserve that the Sagittarian nature sometimes lacks. Although you like to have a good time and would be more than willing to dance the night away, you are probably also happy enough when the time comes to go home. Family means much to you and you have a great sensitivity to the needs of those around you. What makes all the difference is that you not only understand others, but you have the potential to take practical steps to help them.

You are probably not quite the workaholic that the Archer alone tends to be and can gain rest and relaxation, which has to be good for you in the longer term. You don't lack the ability to be successful but your level of application is considered, less frenetic and altogether more ordered. It's true that some confusion comes into your life from time to time, but you have the resources to deal with such eventualities, and you do so with a smile on your face most of the time. People would warm to you almost instantly and you are likely to do whatever you can to support family members and friends.

Often sinking into a dream world if you feel threatened, some of the achievements that are second nature to the Sagittarian are left on the shelf for a while. There are times when this turns out to be a blessing, if only because your actions are more considered. Personality clashes with others are less likely with this combination and Sagittarius also modifies the slightly moody qualities that come with Scorpio alone. More methodical in every way than the usual Archer, in many situations you are a good combination of optimist and pessimist.

The Capricorn Cusp – 19th December to 21st December

The fact that comes across almost immediately with the Capricorn cusp of Sagittarius is how very practical you tend to be. Most of you would be ideal company on a desert island, for a number of reasons. Firstly you are quite self-contained, which Sagittarius taken alone certainly is not. You would soon get your head round the practical difficulties of finding food and shelter, and would be very happy to provide these necessities for your companions too. Unlike the typical Sagittarian you do not boast and probably do not come across as being quite so overbearing as the Archer seems to be. For all this you are friendly, chatty, love to meet many different and interesting types and do whatever you can to be of assistance to a world which is all the better for having you in it.

There is less of a tendency for you to worry at a superficial level than Sagittarius alone is inclined to do, mainly because long periods of practical application bring with them a contemplative tendency that Sagittarius sometimes lacks. In love you tend to be quite sincere, even if the slightly fickle tendencies of the Archer do show through now and again. Any jealousy that is levelled at you by your partner could be as a result of your natural attractiveness, which you probably don't seek. Fairly comfortable in almost any sort of company, you are at your best when faced with individuals who have something intelligent and interesting to say. As a salesperson you would be second to none, but it would be essential for you to believe absolutely in the product or service you were selling.

Almost any sort of work is possible in your case, though you wouldn't take too kindly to being restricted in any way, and need the chance to show what your practical nature is worth, as well as your keen perception and organisational abilities. What matters most for you at work is that you are well liked by others and that you manage to maintain a position of control through inspiring confidence. On a creative level, the combination of Sagittarius and Capricorn would make you a good sculptor, or possibly a natural landscape gardener.

SAGITTARIUS AND ITS ASCENDANTS

The nature of every individual on the planet is composed of the rich variety of zodiac signs and planetary positions that were present at the time of their birth. Your Sun sign, which in your case is Sagittarius, is one of the many factors when it comes to assessing the unique person you are. Probably the most important consideration, other than your Sun sign, is to establish the zodiac sign that was rising over the eastern horizon at the time that you were born. This is your Ascending or Rising sign. Most popular astrology fails to take account of the Ascendant, and yet its importance remains with you from the very moment of your birth, through every day of your life. The Ascendant is evident in the way you approach the world, and so, when meeting a person for the first time, it is this astrological influence that you are most likely to notice first. Our Ascending sign essentially represents what we appear to be, while the Sun sign is what we feel inside ourselves.

The Ascendant also has the potential for modifying our overall nature. For example, if you were born at a time of day when Sagittarius was passing over the eastern horizon (this would be around the time of dawn) then you would be classed as a double Sagittarius. As such, you would typify this zodiac sign, both internally and in your dealings with others. However, if your Ascendant sign turned out to be an Earth sign, such as Taurus, there would be a profound alteration of nature, away from the expected qualities of Sagittarius.

One of the reasons why popular astrology often ignores the Ascendant is that it has always been rather difficult to establish. We have found a way to make this possible by devising an easy-to-use table, which you will find on page 157 of this book. Using this, you can establish your Ascendant sign at a glance. You will need to know your rough time of birth, then it is simply a case of following the instructions.

For those readers who have no idea of their time of birth it might be worth allowing a good friend, or perhaps your partner, to read through the section that follows this introduction. Someone who deals with you on a regular basis may easily discover your Ascending sign, even though you could have some difficulty establishing it for yourself. A good understanding of this component of your nature is essential if you want to be aware of that 'other person' who is responsible for the way you make contact with the world at large. Your Sun sign, Ascendant sign, and the other pointers in this book will, together, allow you a far better understanding of what makes you tick as an individual. Peeling back the different layers of your astrological make-up can be an enlightening experience, and the Ascendant may represent one of the most important layers of all.

Sagittarius with Sagittarius Ascendant

You are very easy to spot, even in a crowd. There is hardly a more dynamic individual to be found anywhere in the length and breadth of the zodiac. You know what you want from life and have a pretty good idea about how you will get it. The fact that you are always so cocksure is a source of great wonder to those around you, but they can't see deep inside, where you are not half as certain as you appear to be. In the main you show yourself to be kind, attentive, caring and a loyal friend. To balance this, you are determined and won't be thwarted by anything.

You keep up a searing pace through life and sometimes find it difficult to understand those people who have slightly less energy. In your better moments you understand that you are unique and will wait for others to catch up. Quite often you need periods of rest in order to recharge batteries that run down through over-use, but it doesn't take you too long to get yourself back on top form. In matters of the heart you can be slightly capricious, but you are a confident lover who knows the right words and gestures. If you are ever accused of taking others for granted you might need to indulge in some self-analysis.

Sagittarius with Capricorn Ascendant

The typical Sagittarian nature is modified for the better when Capricorn is part of the deal. It's true that you manage to push forward progressively under most circumstances, but you also possess staying power and can work long and hard to achieve your objectives, most of which are carefully planned in advance. Few people have the true measure of your nature, for it runs rather deeper than appears to be the case on the surface. Routines don't bother you as much as would be the case for Sagittarius when taken alone, and you don't care if any objective takes weeks, months or even years to achieve. You are very fond of those you take to, and prove to be a capable friend, even when things get tough.

In love relationships you are steadfast and reliable, and yet you never lose the ability to entertain. Yours is a dry sense of humour which shows itself to a multitude of different people and which doesn't evaporate, even on those occasions when life gets tough. It might take you a long time to find the love of your life, but when you do there is a greater possibility of retaining the relationship for a long period. You don't tend to inherit money, but you can easily make it for yourself, though you don't worry too much about the amount. On the whole you are self-sufficient and sensible.

Sagittarius with Aquarius Ascendant

There is an original streak to your nature which is very attractive to the people with whom you share your life. Always different, ever on the go and anxious to try out the next experiment in life, you are interested in almost everything and yet deeply attached to almost nothing. Everyone you know thinks that you are a little 'odd', but you probably don't mind them believing this because you know it to be true. In fact it is possible that you positively relish your eccentricity, which sets you apart from the common herd and means that you are always going to be noticed.

Although it may seem strange with this combination of Air and Fire, you can be distinctly cool on occasions, have a deep and abiding love of your own company now and again, and won't easily be understood. Love comes fairly easily to you but there are times when you are accused of being self-possessed, self-indulgent and not willing enough to fall in line with the wishes of those around you. Despite this you walk on and on down your own path. At heart you are an extrovert and you love to party, often late into the night. Luxury appeals to you, though it tends to be of the transient sort. Travel could easily play a major and a very important part in your life.

Sagittarius with Pisces Ascendant

A very attractive combination this, because the more dominant qualities of the Archer are somehow mellowed-out by the caring Water-sign qualities of the Fishes. You can be very outgoing, but there is always a deeper side to your nature that allows others to know that you are thinking about them. Few people could fall out with either your basic nature or your attitude to the world at large, even though there are depths to your personality that may not be easily understood. You are capable, have a good executive ability and can work hard to achieve your objectives, even if you get a little disillusioned on the way. Much of your life is given over to helping those around you and there is a great tendency for you to work for and on behalf of humanity as a whole. A sense of community is brought to most of what you do and you enjoy co-operation.

Although you have the natural Sagittarian ability to attract people to you, the Pisces half of your nature makes you just a little more reserved in personal matters than might otherwise be the case. More careful in your choices than either sign taken alone, you still have to make certain that your motivations when commencing a personal relationship are the right ones. You love to be happy, and to offer gifts of happiness to others.

Sagittarius with Aries Ascendant

What a lovely combination this can be, for the devil-may-care aspects of Sagittarius lighten the load of a sometimes too serious Aries interior. Everything that glistens is not gold, though it's hard to convince you of the fact because, to mix metaphors, you can make a silk purse out of a sow's ear. Almost everyone loves you, and in return you offer a friendship that is warm and protective, but not as demanding as sometimes tends to be the case with the Aries type. Relationships may be many and varied and there is often more than one major attachment in the life of those holding this combination. You can bring a breath of spring to any relationship, though you need to ensure that the person concerned is capable of keeping up with the hectic pace of your life.

It may appear from time to time that you are rather too trusting for your own good, though deep inside you are very astute, and it seems that almost everything you undertake works out well in the end. This has nothing to do with native luck and is really down to the fact that you are much more calculating than might appear to be the case at first sight. As a parent you are protective, yet offer sufficient room for self-expression.

Sagittarius with Taurus Ascendant

A dual nature is evident here, and if it doesn't serve to confuse you it will certainly be a cause of concern to many of the people with whom you share your life. You like to have a good time and are a natural party-goer. On such occasions you are accommodating, chatty and good to know. But contrast this with the quieter side of Taurus, which is directly opposed to your Sagittarian qualities. The opposition of forces is easy for you to deal with because you inhabit your own body and mind all the time, but it's far less easy for friends and relatives to understand. As a result, on those occasions when you decide that, socially speaking, enough is enough, you will need to explain the fact to the twelve people who are waiting outside your door with party hats and whoopee cushions.

Confidence to do almost anything is not far from the forefront of your mind and you readily embark on adventures that would have some types flapping about in horror. Here again, it is important to realise that we are not all built the same way and that gentle coaxing is sometimes necessary to bring others round to your point of view. If you really have a fault, it could be that you are so busy being your own, rather less than predictable self, that you fail to take the rest of the world into account.

Sagittarius with Gemini Ascendant

'Tomorrow is another day!' This is your belief and you stick to it. There isn't a brighter and more optimistic soul to be found than you and almost everyone you come into contact with is touched by the fact. Dashing about from one place to another, you manage to get more things done in one day than most other people would achieve in a week. Of course this explains why you are so likely to wear yourself out and it means that frequent periods of absolute rest are necessary if you are to remain truly healthy and happy. Sagittarius makes you brave and sometimes a little headstrong, so you need to curb your natural enthusiasm while you stop to think about the consequences of your actions.

It's not really certain if you do 'think' in the accepted sense of the word, because the lightning qualities of both these signs mean that your reactions are second to none. However, you are not indestructible and you put far more pressure on yourself than would often be sensible. Routines are not your thing at all, and many of you manage to hold down two or more jobs at once. It might be an idea to stop and smell the flowers on the way, and you could certainly do with putting your feet up much more than you do. However, you probably won't still be reading this passage because you will have something far more important to do!

Sagittarius with Cancer Ascendant

You have far more drive, enthusiasm and get-up-and-go than would seem to be the case for Cancer when taken alone, but all of this is tempered with a certain quiet compassion that probably makes you the best sort of Sagittarian too. It's true that you don't like to be on your own or to retire in your shell quite as much as the Crab usually does, though there are, even in your case, occasions when this is going to be necessary. Absolute concentration can sometimes be a problem to you, though this is hardly likely to be the case when you are dealing with matters relating to your home or family, both of which reign supreme in your thinking. Always loving and kind, you are a social animal and enjoy being out there in the real world, expressing the deeper opinions of Cancer much more readily than would often be the case with other combinations relating to the sign of the Crab.

Personality is not lacking and you tend to be very popular, not least because you are the fountain of good and practical advice. You want to get things done and retain a practical approach to most situations which is the envy of many other people. As a parent you are second to none, combining common sense, dignity and a sensible approach. To balance this you stay young enough to understand children.

Sagittarius with Leo Ascendant

Above and beyond anything else you are naturally funny, and this is an aspect of your nature that will bring you intact through a whole series of problems that you manage to create for yourself. Chatty, witty, charming, kind and loving, you personify the best qualities of both these signs, whilst also retaining the Fire-sign ability to keep going, long after the rest of the party has gone home to bed. Being great fun to have around, you attract friends in the way that a magnet attracts iron filings. Many of these will be casual connections but there will always be a nucleus of deep, abiding attachments that may stay around you for most of your life.

You don't often suffer from fatigue, but on those occasions when you do there is ample reason to stay still for a while and to take stock of situations. Routines are not your thing and you like to fill your life with variety. It's important to do certain things right, however, and staying power is something that comes with age, assisted by the Fixed quality of Leo. Few would lock horns with you in an argument, which you always have to win. In a way you are a natural debater but you can sometimes carry things too far if you are up against a worthy opponent. You have the confidence to sail through situations that would defeat others.

Sagittarius with Virgo Ascendant

This is a combination that might look rather odd at first sight because these two signs have so very little in common. However, the saying goes that opposites attract, and in terms of the personality you display to the world this is especially true in your case. Not everyone understands what makes you tick but you try to show the least complicated face to the world that you can manage to display. You can be deep and secretive on occasions, and yet at other times you can start talking as soon as you climb out of bed and never stop until you are back there again. Inspirational and spontaneous, you take the world by storm on those occasions when you are free from worries and firing on all cylinders. It is a fact that you support your friends, though there are rather more of them than would be the case for Virgo taken on its own, and you don't always choose them as wisely as you might.

There are times when you display a temper, and although Sagittarius is incapable of bearing a grudge, the same cannot be said for Virgo, which has a better memory than the elephant. For the best results in life you need to relax as much as possible and avoid overheating that powerful and busy brain. Virgo gives you the ability to concentrate on one thing at once, a skill you should encourage.

Sagittarius with Libra Ascendant

A very happy combination this, with a great desire for life in all its forms and a need to push forward the bounds of the possible in a way that few other zodiac sign connections would do. You don't like the unpleasant or ugly in life and yet you are capable of dealing with both if you have to. Giving so much to humanity, you still manage to retain a degree of individuality that would surprise many, charm others, and please all.

On the reverse side of the same coin you might find that you are sometimes accused of being fickle, but this is only an expression of your need for change and variety, which is intrinsic to both these signs. True, you have more of a temper than would be the case for Libra when taken on its own, but such incidents would see you up and down in a flash and it is almost impossible for you to bear a grudge of any sort. Routines get on your nerves and you are far happier when you can please yourself and get ahead at your own pace, which is quite fast.

As a lover you can make a big impression and most of you will not go short of affection in the early days, before you choose to commit yourself. Once you do, there is always a chance of romantic problems, but these are less likely when you have chosen carefully in the first place.

Sagittarius with Scorpio Ascendant

There are many gains with this combination, and most of you reading this will already be familiar with the majority of them. Sagittarius offers a bright and hopeful approach to life, but may not always have the staying power and the patience to get what it really needs. Scorpio, on the other hand, can be too deep for its own good, is very self-seeking on occasions and extremely giving to others. Both the signs have problems when taken on their own, and, it has to be said, double the difficulties when they come together. But this is not usually the case. Invariably the presence of Scorpio slows down the over-quick responses of the Archer, whilst the inclusion of Sagittarius prevents Scorpio from taking itself too seriously.

Life is so often a game of extremes, when all the great spiritual masters of humanity have indicated that a 'middle way' is the path to choose. You have just the right combination of skills and mental faculties to find that elusive path, and can bring great joy to yourself and others as a result. Most of the time you are happy, optimistic, helpful and a joy to know. You have mental agility, backed up by a stunning intuition, which itself would rarely let you down. Keep a sense of proportion and understand that your depth of intellect is necessary in order to curb the more flighty aspects of Scorpio.

THE MOON AND THE PART IT PLAYS IN YOUR LIFE

In astrology the Moon is probably the single most important heavenly body after the Sun. Its unique position, as partner to the Earth on its journey around the solar system, means that the Moon appears to pass through the signs of the zodiac extremely quickly. The zodiac position of the Moon at the time of your birth plays a great part in personal character and is especially significant in the build-up of your emotional nature.

Your Own Moon Sign

Discovering the position of the Moon at the time of your birth has always been notoriously difficult because tracking the complex zodiac positions of the Moon is not easy. This process has been reduced to three simple stages with our Lunar Tables. A breakdown of the Moon's zodiac positions can be found from page 35 onwards, so that once you know what your Moon Sign is, you can see what part this plays in the overall build-up of your personal character.

If you follow the instructions on the next page you will soon be able to work out exactly what zodiac sign the Moon occupied on the day that you were born and you can then go on to compare the reading for this position with those of your Sun sign and your Ascendant. It is partly the comparison between these three important positions that goes towards making you the unique individual you are.

How To Discover Your Moon Sign

This is a three-stage process. You may need a pen and a piece of paper but if you follow the instructions below the process should only take a minute or so.

STAGE 1 First of all you need to know the Moon Age at the time of your birth. If you look at Moon Table 1, on page 33, you will find all the years between 1921 and 2019 down the left side. Find the year of your birth and then trace across to the right to the month of your birth. Where the two intersect you will find a number. This is the date of the New Moon in the month that you were born. You now need to count forward the number of days between the New Moon and your own birthday. For example, if the New Moon in the month of your birth was shown as being the 6th and you were born on the 20th, your Moon Age Day would be 14. If the New Moon in the month of your birth came after your birthday, you need to count forward from the New Moon in the previous month. Whatever the result, jot this number down so that you do not forget it.

STAGE 2 Take a look at Moon Table 2 on page 34. Down the left hand column look for the date of your birth. Now trace across to the month of your birth. Where the two meet you will find a letter. Copy this letter down alongside your Moon Age Day.

STAGE 3 Moon Table 3 on page 34 will supply you with the zodiac sign the Moon occupied on the day of your birth. Look for your Moon Age Day down the left hand column and then for the letter you found in Stage 2. Where the two converge you will find a zodiac sign and this is the sign occupied by the Moon on the day that you were born.

Your Zodiac Moon Sign Explained

You will find a profile of all zodiac Moon Signs on pages 35 to 38, showing in yet another way how astrology helps to make you into the individual that you are. In each daily entry of the Astral Diary you can find the zodiac position of the Moon for every day of the year. This also allows you to discover your lunar birthdays. Since the Moon passes through all the signs of the zodiac in about a month, you can expect something like twelve lunar birthdays each year. At these times you are likely to be emotionally steady and able to make the sort of decisions that have real, lasting value.

MOON TABLE 1

YEAR	OCT	NOV	DEC	YEAR	OCT	NOV	DEC	YEAR	OCT	NOV	DEC
1921	1/30	29	29	1954	26	25	25	1987	22	21	20
1922	20	19	18	1955	15	14	14	1988	10	9	9
1923	10	8	8	1956	4	2	2	1989	29	28	28
1924	28	26	26	1957	23	21	21	1990	18	17	17
1925	17	16	15	1958	12	11	10	1991	8	6	6
1926	6	5	5	1959	2/31	30	29	1992	25	24	24
1927	25	24	24	1960	20	19	18	1993	15	14	14
1928	14	12	12	1961	9	8	7	1994	5	3	2
1929	2	1 1/30		1962	28	27	26	1995	24	22	22
1930	20	19	19	1963	17	15	15	1996	11	10	10
1931	11	9	9	1964	5	4	4	1997	31	30	29
1932	29	27	27	1965	24	22	22	1998	20	19	18
1933	19	17	17	1966	14	12	12	1999	8	8	7
1934	8	7	6	1967	3	2	1/30	2000	27	26	25
1935	27	26	25	1968	22	21	20	2001	17	16	15
1936	15	14	13	1969	10	9	9	2002	6	4	4
1937	4	3	2	1970	1/30	29	28	2003	25	24	23
1938	23	22	21	1971	19	18	17	2004	12	11	11
1939	12	11	10	1972	8	6	6	2005	2	1 1/31	
1940	1/30	29	28	1973	26	25	25	2006	21	20	20
1941	20	19	18	1974	15	14	14	2007	11	9	9
1942	10	8	8	1975	5	3	3	2008	29	28	27
1943	29	27	27	1976	23	21	21	2009	18	17	16
1944	17	15	15	1977	12	11	10	2010	8	6	6
1945	6	4	4	1978	2/31	30	29	2011	27	25	25
1946	24	23	23	1979	20	19	18	2012	15	13	12
1947	14	12	12	1980	9	8	7	2013	4	2	2
1948	2	1 1/30		1981	27	26	26	2014	22	22	1
1949	21	20	19	1982	17	15	15	2015	12	11	20
1950	11	9	9	1983	6	4	4	2016	30	29	29
1951	1/30	29	28	1984	24	22	22	2017	20	18	18
1952	18	17	17	1985	14	12	12	2018	9	7	7
1953	8	6	6	1986	3	2	1/30	2019	27	26	26

TABLE 2   MOON TABLE 3

DAY	NOV	DEC	M/D	e	f	g	i	m	n	q
1	e	i	0	SC	SC	SC	SA	SA	SA	CP
2	e	i	1	SC	SC	SA	SA	SA	CP	CP
3	e	m	2	SC	SA	SA	CP	CP	CP	AQ
4	f	m	3	SA	SA	CP	CP	CP	AQ	AQ
5	f	n	4	SA	CP	CP	CP	AQ	AQ	PI
6	f	n	5	CP	CP	AQ	AQ	AQ	PI	PI
7	f	n	6	CP	AQ	AQ	AQ	AQ	PI	AR
8	f	n	7	AQ	AQ	PI	PI	PI	AR	AR
9	f	n	8	AQ	PI	PI	PI	PI	AR	AR
10	f	n	9	AQ	PI	PI	AR	AR	TA	TA
11	f	n	10	PI	AR	AR	AR	AR	TA	TA
12	f	n	11	PI	AR	AR	TA	TA	TA	GE
13	g	n	12	AR	TA	TA	TA	TA	GE	GE
14	g	n	13	AR	TA	TA	GE	GE	GE	GE
15	g	n	14	TA	GE	GE	GE	GE	CA	CA
16	g	n	15	TA	TA	TA	GE	GE	GE	CA
17	g	n	16	TA	GE	GE	GE	CA	CA	CA
18	g	n	17	GE	GE	GE	CA	CA	CA	LE
19	g	n	18	GE	GE	CA	CA	CA	LE	LE
20	g	n	19	GE	CA	CA	CA	LE	LE	LE
21	g	n	20	CA	CA	CA	LE	LE	LE	VI
22	g	n	21	CA	CA	LE	LE	LE	VI	VI
23	i	q	22	CA	LE	LE	VI	VI	VI	LI
24	i	q	23	LE	LE	LE	VI	VI	VI	LI
25	i	q	24	LE	LE	VI	VI	VI	LI	LI
26	i	q	25	LE	VI	VI	LI	LI	LI	SC
27	i	q	26	VI	VI	LI	LI	LI	SC	SC
28	i	q	27	VI	LI	LI	SC	SC	SC	SA
29	i	q	28	LI	LI	LI	SC	SC	SC	SA
30	i	q	29	LI	LI	SC	SC	SA	SA	SA
31	–	q								

AR = Aries, TA = Taurus, GE = Gemini, CA = Cancer, LE = Leo, VI = Virgo,
LI = Libra, SC = Scorpio, SA = Sagittarius, CP = Capricorn, AQ = Aquarius, PI = Pisces

MOON SIGNS

Moon in Aries

You have a strong imagination, courage, determination and a desire to do things in your own way and forge your own path through life.

Originality is a key attribute; you are seldom stuck for ideas although your mind is changeable and you could take the time to focus on individual tasks. Often quick-tempered, you take orders from few people and live life at a fast pace. Avoid health problems by taking regular time out for rest and relaxation.

Emotionally, it is important that you talk to those you are closest to and work out your true feelings. Once you discover that people are there to help, there is less necessity for you to do everything yourself.

Moon in Taurus

The Moon in Taurus gives you a courteous and friendly manner, which means you are likely to have many friends.

The good things in life mean a lot to you, as Taurus is an Earth sign that delights in experiences which please the senses. Hence you are probably a lover of good food and drink, which may in turn mean you need to keep an eye on the bathroom scales, especially as looking good is also important to you.

Emotionally you are fairly stable and you stick by your own standards. Taureans do not respond well to change. Intuition also plays an important part in your life.

Moon in Gemini

You have a warm-hearted character, sympathetic and eager to help others. At times reserved, you can also be articulate and chatty: this is part of the paradox of Gemini, which always brings duplicity to the nature. You are interested in current affairs, have a good intellect, and are good company and likely to have many friends. Most of your friends have a high opinion of you and would be ready to defend you should the need arise. However, this is usually unnecessary, as you are quite capable of defending yourself in any verbal confrontation.

Travel is important to your inquisitive mind and you find intellectual stimulus in mixing with people from different cultures. You also gain much from reading, writing and the arts but you do need plenty of rest and relaxation in order to avoid fatigue.

Moon in Cancer

The Moon in Cancer at the time of birth is a fortunate position as Cancer is the Moon's natural home. This means that the qualities of compassion and understanding given by the Moon are especially enhanced in your nature, and you are friendly and sociable and cope well with emotional pressures. You cherish home and family life, and happily do the domestic tasks. Your surroundings are important to you and you hate squalor and filth. You are likely to have a love of music and poetry.

Your basic character, although at times changeable like the Moon itself, depends on symmetry. You aim to make your surroundings comfortable and harmonious, for yourself and those close to you.

Moon in Leo

The best qualities of the Moon and Leo come together to make you warm-hearted, fair, ambitious and self-confident. With good organisational abilities, you invariably rise to a position of responsibility in your chosen career. This is fortunate as you don't enjoy being an 'also-ran' and would rather be an important part of a small organisation than a menial in a large one.

You should be lucky in love, and happy, provided you put in the effort to make a comfortable home for yourself and those close to you. It is likely that you will have a love of pleasure, sport, music and literature. Life brings you many rewards, most of them as a direct result of your own efforts, although you may be luckier than average and ready to make the best of any situation.

Moon in Virgo

You are endowed with good mental abilities and a keen receptive memory, but you are never ostentatious or pretentious. Naturally quite reserved, you still have many friends, especially of the opposite sex. Marital relationships must be discussed carefully and worked at so that they remain harmonious, as personal attachments can be a problem if you do not give them your full attention.

Talented and persevering, you possess artistic qualities and are a good homemaker. Earning your honours through genuine merit, you work long and hard towards your objectives but show little pride in your achievements. Many short journeys will be undertaken in your life.

Moon in Libra

With the Moon in Libra you are naturally popular and make friends easily. People like you, probably more than you realise, you bring fun to a party and are a natural diplomat. For all its good points, Libra is not the most stable of astrological signs and, as a result, your emotions can be a little unstable too. Therefore, although the Moon in Libra is said to be good for love and marriage, your Sun sign and Rising sign will have an important effect on your emotional and loving qualities.

You must remember to relate to others in your decision-making. Co-operation is crucial because Libra represents the 'balance' of life that can only be achieved through harmonious relationships. Conformity is not easy for you because Libra, an Air sign, likes its independence.

Moon in Scorpio

Some people might call you pushy. In fact, all you really want to do is to live life to the full and protect yourself and your family from the pressures of life. Take care to avoid giving the impression of being sarcastic or impulsive and use your energies wisely and constructively.

You have great courage and you invariably achieve your goals by force of personality and sheer effort. You are fond of mystery and are good at predicting the outcome of situations and events. Travel experiences can be beneficial to you.

You may experience problems if you do not take time to examine your motives in a relationship, and also if you allow jealousy, always a feature of Scorpio, to cloud your judgement.

Moon in Sagittarius

The Moon in Sagittarius helps to make you a generous individual with humanitarian qualities and a kind heart. Restlessness may be intrinsic as your mind is seldom still. Perhaps because of this, you have a need for change that could lead you to several major moves during your adult life. You are not afraid to stand your ground when you know your judgement is right, you speak directly and have good intuition.

At work you are quick, efficient and versatile and so you make an ideal employee. You need work to be intellectually demanding and do not enjoy tedious routines.

In relationships, you anger quickly if faced with stupidity or deception, though you are just as quick to forgive and forget. Emotionally, there are times when your heart rules your head.

Moon in Capricorn

The Moon in Capricorn makes you popular and likely to come into the public eye in some way. The watery Moon is not entirely comfortable in the Earth sign of Capricorn and this may lead to some difficulties in the early years of life. An initial lack of creative ability and indecision must be overcome before the true qualities of patience and perseverance inherent in Capricorn can show through.

You have good administrative ability and are a capable worker, and if you are careful you can accumulate wealth. But you must be cautious and take professional advice in partnerships, as you are open to deception. You may be interested in social or welfare work, which suit your organisational skills and sympathy for others.

Moon in Aquarius

The Moon in Aquarius makes you an active and agreeable person with a friendly, easy-going nature. Sympathetic to the needs of others, you flourish in a laid-back atmosphere. You are broad-minded, fair and open to suggestion, although sometimes you have an unconventional quality which others can find hard to understand.

You are interested in the strange and curious, and in old articles and places. You enjoy trips to these places and gain much from them. Political, scientific and educational work interests you and you might choose a career in science or technology.

Money-wise, you make gains through innovation and concentration and Lunar Aquarians often tackle more than one job at a time. In love you are kind and honest.

Moon in Pisces

You have a kind, sympathetic nature, somewhat retiring at times, but you always take account of others' feelings and help when you can.

Personal relationships may be problematic, but as life goes on you can learn from your experiences and develop a better understanding of yourself and the world around you.

You have a fondness for travel, appreciate beauty and harmony and hate disorder and strife. You may be fond of literature and would make a good writer or speaker yourself. You have a creative imagination and may come across as an incurable romantic. You have strong intuition, maybe bordering on a mediumistic quality, which sets you apart from the mass. You may not be rich in cash terms, but your personal gifts are worth more than gold.

SAGITTARIUS IN LOVE

Discover how compatible in love you are with people from the same and other signs of the zodiac. Five stars equals a match made in heaven!

Sagittarius meets Sagittarius

Although perhaps not the very best partnership for Sagittarius, this must rank as one of the most eventful, electrifying and interesting of the bunch. They will think alike, which is often the key to any relationship but, unfortunately, they may be so busy leading their own lives that they don't spend much time together. Their social life should be something special, and there could be lots of travel. However, domestic responsibilities need to be carefully shared and the family might benefit from a helping hand in this area. Star rating: ****

Sagittarius meets Capricorn

Any real problem here will stem from a lack of understanding. Capricorn is very practical and needs to be constantly on the go, though in a fairly low-key sort of way. Sagittarius is busy too, though always in a panic and invariably behind its deadlines, which will annoy organised Capricorn. Sagittarius doesn't really have the depth of nature that best suits an Earth sign like Capricorn and its flirty nature could upset the sensitive Goat, though its lighter attitude could be cheering, too. Star rating: ***

Sagittarius meets Aquarius

Both Sagittarius and Aquarius are into mind games, which may lead to something of an intellectual competition. If one side is happy to be bamboozled it won't be a problem, but it is more likely that the relationship will turn into a competition which won't auger well for its long-term future. However, on the plus side, both signs are adventurous and sociable, so as long as there is always something new and interesting to do, the match could end up turning out very well. Star rating: **

Sagittarius meets Pisces

Probably the least likely success story for either sign, which is why it scores so low on the star rating. The basic problem is an almost total lack of understanding. A successful relationship needs empathy and progress towards a shared goal but, although both are eager to please, Pisces is too deep and Sagittarius too flighty – they just don't belong on the same planet! As pals, they have more in common and so a friendship is the best hope of success and happiness. Star rating: *

Sagittarius meets Aries

This can be one of the most favourable matches of them all. Both Aries and Sagittarius are Fire signs, which often leads to clashes of will, but this pair find a mutual understanding. Sagittarius helps Aries to develop a better sense of humour, while Aries teaches the Archer about consistency on the road to success. Some patience is called for on both sides, but these people have a natural liking for each other. Add this to growing love and you have a long-lasting combination that is hard to beat. Star rating: *****

Sagittarius meets Taurus

On first impression, Taurus may not like Sagittarius, which may seem brash, and even common, when viewed through the Bull's refined eyes. But, there is hope of success because the two signs have so much to offer each other. The Archer is enthralled by the Taurean's natural poise and beauty, while Taurus always needs more basic confidence, which is no problem to Sagittarius who has plenty to spare. Both signs love to travel. There are certain to be ups and downs, but that doesn't prevent an interesting, inspiring and even exciting combination. Star rating: ***

Sagittarius meets Gemini

A paradoxical relationship this. On paper, the two signs have much in common, but unfortunately, they are often so alike that life turns into a fiercely fought competition. Both signs love change and diversity and both want to be the life and soul of the party. But in life there must always be a leader and a follower, and neither of this pair wants to be second. Both also share a tendency towards infidelity, which may develop into a problem as time passes. This could be an interesting match, but not necessarily successful. Star rating: **

Sagittarius meets Cancer

Although probably not an immediate success, there is hope for this couple. It's hard to see how this pair could get together, because they have few mutual interests. Sagittarius is always on the go, loves a hectic social life and dances the night away. Cancer prefers the cinema or a concert. But, having met, Cancer will appreciate the Archer's happy and cheerful nature, while Sagittarius finds Cancer alluring and intriguing and, as the saying goes, opposites attract. A long-term relationship would focus on commitment to family, with Cancer leading this area. Star rating: ***

Sagittarius meets Leo

An excellent match as Leo and Sagittarius have so much in common. Their general approach to life is very similar, although as they are both Fire signs they can clash impressively! Sagittarius is shallower and more flippant than Leo likes to think of itself, and the Archer will be the one taking emotional chances. Sagittarius has met its match in the Lion's den, as brave Leo won't be outdone by anyone. Financially, they will either be very wealthy or struggling, and family life may be chaotic. Problems, like joys, are handled jointly – and that leads to happiness. Star rating: *****

Sagittarius meets Virgo

There can be some quite strange happenings inside this relationship. Sagittarius and Virgo view life so differently there are always new discoveries. Virgo is much more of a home-bird than Sagittarius, but that won't matter if the Archer introduces its hectic social life gradually. More importantly, Sagittarius understands that it takes Virgo a long time to free its hidden 'inner sprite', but once free it will be fun all the way – until Virgo's thrifty nature takes over. There are great possibilities, but effort is required. Star rating: ***

Sagittarius meets Libra

Libra and Sagittarius are both adaptable signs who get on well with most people, but this promising outlook often does not follow through because each brings out the 'flighty' side of the other. This combination is great for a fling, but when the romance is over someone needs to see to the practical side of life. Both signs are well meaning, pleasant and kind, but are either of them constant enough to build a life together? In at least some cases, the answer would be no. Star rating: ***

Sagittarius meets Scorpio

Sagittarius needs constant stimulation and loves to be busy from dawn till dusk which may mean that it feels rather frustrated by Scorpio. Scorpions are hard workers, too, but they are also contemplative and need periods of quiet which may mean that they appear dull to Sagittarius. This could lead to a gulf between the two which must be overcome. With time and patience on both sides, this can be a lucrative encounter and good in terms of home and family. A variable alliance. Star rating: ***

VENUS:
THE PLANET OF LOVE

If you look up at the sky around sunset or sunrise you will often see Venus in close attendance to the Sun. It is arguably one of the most beautiful sights of all and there is little wonder that historically it became associated with the goddess of love. But although Venus does play an important part in the way you view love and in the way others see you romantically, this is only one of the spheres of influence that it enjoys in your overall character.

Venus has a part to play in the more cultured side of your life and has much to do with your appreciation of art, literature, music and general creativity. Even the way you look is responsive to the part of the zodiac that Venus occupied at the start of your life, though this fact is also down to your Sun sign and Ascending sign. If, at the time you were born, Venus occupied one of the more gregarious zodiac signs, you will be more likely to wear your heart on your sleeve, as well as to be more attracted to entertainment, social gatherings and good company. If on the other hand Venus occupied a quiet zodiac sign at the time of your birth, you would tend to be more retiring and less willing to shine in public situations.

It's good to know what part the planet Venus plays in your life for it can have a great bearing on the way you appear to the rest of the world and since we all have to mix with others, you can learn to make the very best of what Venus has to offer you.

One of the great complications in the past has always been trying to establish exactly what zodiac position Venus enjoyed when you were born because the planet is notoriously difficult to track. However, we have solved that problem by creating a table that is exclusive to your Sun sign, which you will find on the following page.

Establishing your Venus sign could not be easier. Just look up the year of your birth on the following page and you will see a sign of the zodiac. This was the sign that Venus occupied in the period covered by your sign in that year. If Venus occupied more than one sign during the period, this is indicated by the date on which the sign changed, and the name of the new sign. For instance, if you were born in 1950, Venus was in Sagittarius until the 16th December, after which time it was in Capricorn. If you were born before 16th December your Venus sign is Sagittarius, if you were born on or after 16th December, your Venus sign is Capricorn. Once you have established the position of Venus at the time of your birth, you can then look in the pages which follow to see how this has a bearing on your life as a whole.

1921 SCORPIO / 7.12 SAGITTARIUS
1922 SAGITTARIUS / 29.11 SCORPIO
1923 SAGITTARIUS / 2.12 CAPRICORN
1924 LIBRA / 27.11 SCORPIO
1925 CAPRICORN / 6.12 AQUARIUS
1926 SAGITTARIUS /
    17.12 CAPRICORN
1927 LIBRA / 9.12 SCORPIO
1928 CAPRICORN / 13.12 AQUARIUS
1929 SCORPIO / 7.12 SAGITTARIUS
1930 SCORPIO
1931 SAGITTARIUS / 2.12 CAPRICORN
1932 LIBRA / 26.11 SCORPIO
1933 CAPRICORN / 6.12 AQUARIUS
1934 SAGITTARIUS /
    17.12 CAPRICORN
1935 LIBRA / 10.12 SCORPIO
1936 CAPRICORN / 12.12 AQUARIUS
1937 SCORPIO / 6.12 SAGITTARIUS
1938 SCORPIO
1939 SAGITTARIUS / 1.12 CAPRICORN
1940 LIBRA / 26.11 SCORPIO
1941 CAPRICORN / 6.12 AQUARIUS
1942 SAGITTARIUS /
    16.12 CAPRICORN
1943 LIBRA / 10.12 SCORPIO
1944 CAPRICORN / 12.12 AQUARIUS
1945 SCORPIO / 6.12 SAGITTARIUS
1946 SCORPIO
1947 SAGITTARIUS / 1.12 CAPRICORN
1948 LIBRA / 25.11 SCORPIO /
    20.12 SAGITTARIUS
1949 CAPRICORN / 7.12 AQUARIUS
1950 SAGITTARIUS /
    16.12 CAPRICORN
1951 LIBRA / 10.12 SCORPIO
1952 CAPRICORN / 11.12 AQUARIUS
1953 SCORPIO / 5.12 SAGITTARIUS
1954 SCORPIO
1955 SAGITTARIUS /
    30.11 CAPRICORN
1956 LIBRA / 25.11 SCORPIO /
20.12 SAGITTARIUS
1957 CAPRICORN / 8.12 AQUARIUS
1958 SAGITTARIUS /
    15.12 CAPRICORN
1959 LIBRA / 10.12 SCORPIO
1960 CAPRICORN / 11.12 AQUARIUS
1961 SCORPIO / 5.12 SAGITTARIUS
1962 SCORPIO
1963 SAGITTARIUS /
    30.11 CAPRICORN
1964 LIBRA / 24.11 SCORPIO /
    19.12 SAGITTARIUS
1965 CAPRICORN / 8.12 AQUARIUS
1966 SAGITTARIUS /
    15.12 CAPRICORN
1967 LIBRA / 10.12 SCORPIO
1968 CAPRICORN / 10.12 AQUARIUS
1969 SCORPIO / 4.12 SAGITTARIUS
1970 SCORPIO
1971 SAGITTARIUS /
    29.11 CAPRICORN

1972 LIBRA / 24.11 SCORPIO /
    19.12 SAGITTARIUS
1973 CAPRICORN / 9.12 AQUARIUS
1974 SAGITTARIUS /
    14.12 CAPRICORN
1975 LIBRA / 9.12 SCORPIO
1976 CAPRICORN / 9.12 AQUARIUS
1977 SCORPIO / 4.12 SAGITTARIUS
1978 SCORPIO
1979 SAGITTARIUS /
    28.11 CAPRICORN
1980 SCORPIO / 18.12 SAGITTARIUS
1981 CAPRICORN / 10.12 AQUARIUS
1982 SAGITTARIUS /
    14.12 CAPRICORN
1983 LIBRA / 9.12 SCORPIO
1984 CAPRICORN / 9.12 AQUARIUS
1985 SCORPIO / 3.12 SAGITTARIUS
1986 SCORPIO
1987 SAGITTARIUS /
    28.11 CAPRICORN
1988 SCORPIO / 18.12 SAGITTARIUS
1989 CAPRICORN / 11.12 AQUARIUS
1990 SAGITTARIUS /
    13.12 CAPRICORN
1991 LIBRA / 9.12 SCORPIO
1992 CAPRICORN / 9.12 AQUARIUS
1993 SCORPIO / 3.12 SAGITTARIUS
1994 SCORPIO
1995 SAGITTARIUS /
    28.11 CAPRICORN
1996 SCORPIO / 17.12 SAGITTARIUS
1997 CAPRICORN / 12.12 AQUARIUS
1998 SAGITTARIUS /
    13.12 CAPRICORN
1999 LIBRA / 9.12 SCORPIO
2000 CAPRICORN / 8.12 AQUARIUS
2001 SCORPIO / 3.12 SAGITTARIUS
2002 SCORPIO
2003 SAGITTARIUS/28.11 CAPRICORN
2004 SCORPIO / 17.12 SAGITTARIUS
2005 CAPRICORN / 12.12 AQUARIUS
2006 SAGITTARIUS / 13.12
    CAPRICORN
2007 LIBRA / 9.12 SCORPIO
2008 CAPRICORN / 8.12 AQUARIUS
2009 SCORPIO / 3.12 AQUARIUS
2010 SCORPIO
2011 SAGITTARIUS /
    28.11 CAPRICORN
2012 SCORPIO / 17.12 SAGITTARIUS
2013 SAGITTARIUS /
    13.12 CAPRICORN
2014 SAGITTARIUS /
    13.12 CAPRICORN
2015 LIBRA / 9.12 SCORPIO
2016 CAPRICORN / 8.12 AQUARIUS
2017 SCORPIO / 3.12 AQUARIUS
2018 SCORPIO
2019 SAGITTARIUS/
    28.11 CAPRICORN

44

VENUS THROUGH THE ZODIAC SIGNS

Venus in Aries

Amongst other things, the position of Venus in Aries indicates a fondness for travel, music and all creative pursuits. Your nature tends to be affectionate and you would try not to create confusion or difficulty for others if it could be avoided. Many people with this planetary position have a great love of the theatre, and mental stimulation is of the greatest importance. Early romantic attachments are common with Venus in Aries, so it is very important to establish a genuine sense of romantic continuity. Early marriage is not recommended, especially if it is based on sympathy. You may give your heart a little too readily on occasions.

Venus in Taurus

You are capable of very deep feelings and your emotions tend to last for a very long time. This makes you a trusting partner and lover, whose constancy is second to none. In life you are precise and careful and always try to do things the right way. Although this means an ordered life, which you are comfortable with, it can also lead you to be rather too fussy for your own good. Despite your pleasant nature, you are very fixed in your opinions and quite able to speak your mind. Others are attracted to you and historical astrologers always quoted this position of Venus as being very fortunate in terms of marriage. However, if you find yourself involved in a failed relationship, it could take you a long time to trust again.

Venus in Gemini

As with all associations related to Gemini, you tend to be quite versatile, anxious for change and intelligent in your dealings with the world at large. You may gain money from more than one source but you are equally good at spending it. There is an inference here that you are a good communicator, via either the written or the spoken word, and you love to be in the company of interesting people. Always on the look-out for culture, you may also be very fond of music, and love to indulge the curious and cultured side of your nature. In romance you tend to have more than one relationship and could find yourself associated with someone who has previously been a friend or even a distant relative.

Venus in Cancer

You often stay close to home because you are very fond of family and enjoy many of your most treasured moments when you are with those you love. Being naturally sympathetic, you will always do anything you can to support those around you, even people you hardly know at all. This charitable side of your nature is your most noticeable trait and is one of the reasons why others are naturally so fond of you. Being receptive and in some cases even psychic, you can see through to the soul of most of those with whom you come into contact. You may not commence too many romantic attachments but when you do give your heart, it tends to be unconditionally.

Venus in Leo

It must become quickly obvious to almost anyone you meet that you are kind, sympathetic and yet determined enough to stand up for anyone or anything that is truly important to you. Bright and sunny, you warm the world with your natural enthusiasm and would rarely do anything to hurt those around you, or at least not intentionally. In romance you are ardent and sincere, though some may find your style just a little overpowering. Gains come through your contacts with other people and this could be especially true with regard to romance, for love and money often come hand in hand for those who were born with Venus in Leo. People claim to understand you, though you are more complex than you seem.

Venus in Virgo

Your nature could well be fairly quiet no matter what your Sun sign might be, though this fact often manifests itself as an inner peace and would not prevent you from being basically sociable. Some delays and even the odd disappointment in love cannot be ruled out with this planetary position, though it's a fact that you will usually find the happiness you look for in the end. Catapulting yourself into romantic entanglements that you know to be rather ill-advised is not sensible, and it would be better to wait before you committed yourself exclusively to any one person. It is the essence of your nature to serve the world at large and through doing so it is possible that you will attract money at some stage in your life.

Venus in Libra

Venus is very comfortable in Libra and bestows upon those people who have this planetary position a particular sort of kindness that is easy to recognise. This is a very good position for all sorts of friendships and also for romantic attachments that usually bring much joy into your life. Few individuals with Venus in Libra would avoid marriage and since you are capable of great depths of love, it is likely that you will find a contented personal life. You like to mix with people of integrity and intelligence but don't take kindly to scruffy surroundings or work that means getting your hands too dirty. Careful speculation, good business dealings and money through marriage all seem fairly likely.

Venus in Scorpio

You are quite open and tend to spend money quite freely, even on those occasions when you don't have very much. Although your intentions are always good, there are times when you get yourself in to the odd scrape and this can be particularly true when it comes to romance, which you may come to late or from a rather unexpected direction. Certainly you have the power to be happy and to make others contented on the way, but you find the odd stumbling block on your journey through life and it could seem that you have to work harder than those around you. As a result of this, you gain a much deeper understanding of the true value of personal happiness than many people ever do, and are likely to achieve true contentment in the end.

Venus in Sagittarius

You are lighthearted, cheerful and always able to see the funny side of any situation. These facts enhance your popularity, which is especially high with members of the opposite sex. You should never have to look too far to find romantic interest in your life, though it is just possible that you might be too willing to commit yourself before you are certain that the person in question is right for you. Part of the problem here extends to other areas of life too. The fact is that you like variety in everything and so can tire of situations that fail to offer it. All the same, if you choose wisely and learn to understand your restless side, then great happiness can be yours.

Venus in Capricorn

The most notable trait that comes from Venus in this position is that it makes you trustworthy and able to take on all sorts of responsibilities in life. People are instinctively fond of you and love you all the more because you are always ready to help those who are in any form of need. Social and business popularity can be yours and there is a magnetic quality to your nature that is particularly attractive in a romantic sense. Anyone who wants a partner for a lover, a spouse and a good friend too would almost certainly look in your direction. Constancy is the hallmark of your nature and unfaithfulness would go right against the grain. You might sometimes be a little too trusting.

Venus in Aquarius

This location of Venus offers a fondness for travel and a desire to try out something new at every possible opportunity. You are extremely easy to get along with and tend to have many friends from varied backgrounds, classes and inclinations. You like to live a distinct sort of life and gain a great deal from moving about, both in a career sense and with regard to your home. It is not out of the question that you could form a romantic attachment to someone who comes from far away or be attracted to a person of a distinctly artistic and original nature. What you cannot stand is jealousy, for you have friends of both sexes and would want to keep things that way.

Venus in Pisces

The first thing people tend to notice about you is your wonderful, warm smile. Being very charitable by nature you will do anything to help others, even if you don't know them well. Much of your life may be spent sorting out situations for other people, but it is very important to feel that you are living for yourself too. In the main, you remain cheerful, and tend to be quite attractive to members of the opposite sex. Where romantic attachments are concerned, you could be drawn to people who are significantly older or younger than yourself or to someone with a unique career or point of view. It might be best for you to avoid marrying whilst you are still very young.

SAGITTARIUS:
2018 DIARY PAGES

October

2018

1 MONDAY
Moon Age Day 22   Moon Sign Gemini

Now the lunar low is well under way and this coincides with the start of a new working week. It would be advisable to move slowly and cautiously today and not to get too involved in situations you don't really understand. Learning on the job is part of what Sagittarius is about but the technique may not work too well for the moment.

2 TUESDAY
Moon Age Day 23   Moon Sign Cancer

In professional relationships it is now important for you to cultivate a more tolerant attitude. It could be that people are doing things that seem certain to irritate you though part of the problem could be coming from you. No such worries seem to exist in a more personal sense. You are warm and loving for most of the time.

3 WEDNESDAY
Moon Age Day 24   Moon Sign Cancer

Now you are especially sensitive regarding the impression you make on those around you – and much more so than would generally be the case. This does have a down side because for much of today it could feel as though you are walking on eggshells. Perhaps you are worrying too much. People are more resilient than you think.

4 THURSDAY
Moon Age Day 25   Moon Sign Leo

Your strengths today lie in love and all romantic matters. You have all it takes to be wonderful in the eyes of someone you count as being very special. For those Sagittarians who are not in a relationship at the moment it would be worth keeping your eyes open because Cupid is definitely about.

5 FRIDAY
Moon Age Day 26   Moon Sign Leo

Focus your sights on the romantic arena because you are still well able to turn heads and the effect you have on others is noteworthy. Part of the reason for this is your ability to become whatever is necessary under any given circumstance. Leopards might not be able to change their spots but for an Archer it is child's play.

6 SATURDAY
Moon Age Day 27   Moon Sign Virgo

You may now begin to enjoy a new sense of freedom. There could be less clutter in your life, partly brought about by your ability to ignore or dispose of issues that are no longer relevant to you. If you find yourself involved in any situation that involves confrontation you could discover that you are somewhat braver than you realised.

7 SUNDAY
Moon Age Day 28   Moon Sign Virgo

When it comes to the practical side of life there is a sense that new things are happening all the time. This keeps you involved and interested, which is far better than allowing yourself to become bored with the same old routines. If you had begun to slightly doubt your popularity today's evidence should set you straight.

8 MONDAY
Moon Age Day 29   Moon Sign Virgo

Opportunities now exist to get ahead in job-related matters. At the same time there is just a chance that you are getting carried away with your own sense of purpose and you won't suffer fools gladly. The only problem lies in the fact that all the judgements are yours and it might turn out that someone is not being in the least foolish.

9 TUESDAY
Moon Age Day 0   Moon Sign Libra

Increased activity in your social life mirrors what is taking place at work and, all in all, you are likely to be getting busier and busier. That's fine as long as you don't run yourself ragged in your desire to achieve everything that is possible. Try to find time today to get in touch with friends who might have slipped from sight of late.

10 WEDNESDAY   *Moon Age Day 1   Moon Sign Libra*

If you want to make some of your dreams into reality you are now in the best possible position to do so. People close to you should be more than happy to lend a hand and they will also be willing to share some of your erstwhile fantasies. Travel may be uppermost in your mind and get out and about freely today.

11 THURSDAY   *Moon Age Day 2   Moon Sign Scorpio*

Do whatever you think is necessary today in order to get important people on your side. You are in a good position to get ahead in the practical world and all you need to complete the picture is a leg up from someone who has influence. Your charming nature should take care of the details and the rest is just a matter of flattery.

12 FRIDAY   *Moon Age Day 3   Moon Sign Scorpio*

Right now there is a positive focus on material issues. You can build on fresh starts and will be able to demonstrate that you are certainly not a one-trick pony. Take note of good advice from friends and also try to put some time aside today to let your partner know you haven't entirely forgotten that they exist!

13 SATURDAY   *Moon Age Day 4   Moon Sign Sagittarius*

Act now and ask questions later. It's true that the Archer is sometimes too inclined to be impetuous but, for once, that should turn out to be a good thing. The lunar high means you will be charm itself and you are well able to get what you want when you need it. Good fortune is also likely to be on your side today and tomorrow at least.

14 SUNDAY   *Moon Age Day 5   Moon Sign Sagittarius*

You now have energy in abundance and no shortage of situations in which to use it throughout the whole day. People warm to your infectious enthusiasm and will be quite happy to be carried along with you. Not everything you dream up today will be practical in the longer-term but some of your ideas could run.

15 MONDAY · *Moon Age Day 6 · Moon Sign Capricorn*

Your tendency to be impulsive in your approach to others might take you just a little too far today, unless you exercise some control. There is a fine line between getting what you want and pushing people too hard. In most circumstances you walk that line with consummate professionalism but right now there is a chance you could fall off.

16 TUESDAY · *Moon Age Day 7 · Moon Sign Capricorn*

A mixture of tact and confidence makes your approach to others so good that they could hardly refuse you any reasonable request. As a result this is the best day of the week to ask for something you want – maybe a rise in salary or different working conditions. In any situation where you are explaining yourself you positively shine.

17 WEDNESDAY · *Moon Age Day 8 · Moon Sign Capricorn*

It looks as though you will be extremely busy today and won't have quite as much time to spend counselling others as both they and you might wish. All the same you will need to find a few moments to look after the interests of family members, as well as showing them that their needs and concerns are well understood.

18 THURSDAY · *Moon Age Day 9 · Moon Sign Aquarius*

There are good times on the way when it comes to getting on well at work. Some Sagittarians might be thinking about a total change of career but this may turn out to be unnecessary. The one thing you don't need this month is to become bored with your lot in life. Find some way to bring more excitement to your daily routines.

19 FRIDAY · *Moon Age Day 10 · Moon Sign Aquarius*

You won't want to do anything that goes against the grain today and will be quite happy to simply potter about in a way that suits you. That's fine as far as it goes but it doesn't take account of necessary responsibilities and the needs family members have of you. In some situations you will be far too casual and inclined to shrug things off.

20 SATURDAY   *Moon Age Day 11   Moon Sign Pisces*

Look carefully at your finances this weekend and make any minor adjustments that seem necessary. For today you are active and enterprising but changes are on the way and so avoid taking on too much if it means putting in extra effort. Put a full stop to some issues right now.

21 SUNDAY   *Moon Age Day 12   Moon Sign Pisces*

Sunday positively demands that you have fun and that you take other people with you on the roller coaster ride that is the Archer's life. For their part they should be more than willing to join in and there ought to be many laughs today. Socially and romantically you appear to have everything well sorted out.

22 MONDAY   *Moon Age Day 13   Moon Sign Pisces*

There is no shortage of tasks to get your teeth into at the start of this week and you should be filled with a desire to get everything possible done. Of course there may be moments when you have to stop and think more clearly about specific issues, so rushing all the time could prove to be a negative approach.

23 TUESDAY   *Moon Age Day 14   Moon Sign Aries*

Now fully committed to either career or education you learn quickly, adapt instantly and make the best of impressions on just about anyone. It will be necessary to do the things you don't want to do first – before you embark upon more enjoyable pursuits. Start early in the day and then you will have plenty of time for everything.

24 WEDNESDAY   *Moon Age Day 15   Moon Sign Aries*

You can now be an inspiration to others and show by your attitudes and actions that you are a worthy role model. Avoid family arguments or even disputes with friends because once you start arguing now it is difficult for you to stop. Not everything is going to go your way on this particular Wednesday but the horizon looks good.

25 THURSDAY   *Moon Age Day 16   Moon Sign Taurus*

The slightest thing you do for those around you is likely to be noticed and could be blown up out of all proportion as far as you are concerned. Nevertheless you will be popular and the social invitations are likely to roll in as a result. What you might really need is a rest but that can come later. For the moment just enjoy yourself.

26 FRIDAY   *Moon Age Day 17   Moon Sign Taurus*

Give yourself fully to one task at a time and everything should turn out just fine. What you don't need is to have to start jobs all over again because they were not done properly. What's more you are being carefully monitored at present and will give a better impression of yourself if it is seen that you are efficient and exacting.

27 SATURDAY   *Moon Age Day 18   Moon Sign Gemini*

You are unlikely to be up for new challenges now and will be happiest when you can simply plod along at your own chosen pace. The lunar low is almost certain to make you more emotionally responsive and you could feel as if there is nothing ahead that appears exciting. Don't react too strongly to what is a minor blip and nothing more.

28 SUNDAY   *Moon Age Day 19   Moon Sign Gemini*

Perhaps you are still not giving of your best or feeling satisfied with life. As a result you could be moody and inclined to be pessimistic which is most unlike Sagittarius. Don't worry – very soon the clouds will clear, the lunar low will pass and a new week will bring an entirely different approach.

29 MONDAY   *Moon Age Day 20   Moon Sign Cancer*

What really sets you apart at the moment is your huge and all-encompassing heart. Anyone who is in trouble or who needs timely advice could well be turning in your direction and will be grateful for your input. It might be suggested that the Archer is much better at sorting out the lives of others than it is at dealing with its own.

30 TUESDAY   *Moon Age Day 21   Moon Sign Cancer*

Affairs of the heart are well accented under present trends and you should easily be able to make the sort of first impression for which Sagittarius is famous. Whoever you encounter today it will be possible for you to weigh up the pros and cons of their nature and to react accordingly. You should also be quite sporting around now.

31 WEDNESDAY   *Moon Age Day 22   Moon Sign Cancer*

Some extra care is necessary over decisions at work, though socially it looks as though you are pushing ahead progressively and making a good impression on almost everyone. The result could be a series of new friends or an association with a group that hasn't played an important part in your life up to now.

November
2018

1 THURSDAY
Moon Age Day 23   Moon Sign Leo

Things are likely to be especially busy around your home and there might not be as much time as you would wish to commit yourself to the world outside. Relatives could be quite demanding and it won't be easy to fulfil everyone's expectations. Try to ring the changes as far as your social life is concerned.

2 FRIDAY
Moon Age Day 24   Moon Sign Leo

Take any opportunity that comes along to express yourself fully because otherwise there is a chance that people will fail to understand your reasoning or motivations. You can't be too truthful at the present time, even if you are a little worried that someone might think you are irrational or over-hasty.

3 SATURDAY
Moon Age Day 25   Moon Sign Virgo

Stand up for what you believe to be true and people will respect you much more than you might think. This weekend you could be faced with issues that need a swift resolution and nobody is better equipped to deal with the moment than you are. Look for a potentially warm and romantic evening to end a positive day.

4 SUNDAY
Moon Age Day 26   Moon Sign Virgo

Some personal attachments might seem to be more trouble than they are worth just at present. Of course this isn't really the case but it is true that even your partner might be causing you a degree of anxiety. Talk things through and accept that others may have a viewpoint that is sometimes far from your own. All that is needed is patience.

57

5 MONDAY · *Moon Age Day 27 · Moon Sign Libra*

The interest you show in other people is noteworthy at the best of times but at the moment it is amazing. Nothing passes you by today and every nuance of life falls under your scrutiny. Some people might say you are nosey but in reality you only want to know what makes situations so fascinating and, of course, so diverse.

6 TUESDAY · *Moon Age Day 28 · Moon Sign Libra*

Career and professional objectives are much more likely to come to fruition than personal ones and you won't have any real difficulty getting your message across at work. Most Sagittarians will now show themselves to be capable and well able to shoulder new responsibilities. However, not all colleagues will be on your side.

7 WEDNESDAY · *Moon Age Day 0 · Moon Sign Scorpio*

As always you are very tolerant towards those around you. Your 'live and let live' approach means that you rarely attract enemies but it can also get you accused on occasions of having no moral standards. This is not the case at all and you can prove at the moment how very human and humane you really are.

8 THURSDAY · *Moon Age Day 1 · Moon Sign Scorpio*

You have a talent for working in a one-to-one environment and you will be at your best today when you have to co-operate in order to make things work. There are times when you could be a little more competitive because you are sometimes too willing to settle for compromise all round. Finding the right balance is what today demands.

9 FRIDAY · *Moon Age Day 2 · Moon Sign Sagittarius*

Today the Moon returns to your zodiac sign and the lunar high offers all sorts of new incentives and possibilities you hadn't noticed before. Fortune takes you by the hand and guides you in the right direction and you are likely to be filled with a sense of fun from morning until night. You might confuse the lives of others but not your own.

10 SATURDAY *Moon Age Day 3 Moon Sign Sagittarius*

With boundless energy and a great determination to do everything you can to get ahead it is going to take people with real vitality to stay the course with you. Don't be too quick to point out the faults of others, especially since you might inadvertently be criticising yourself too. Keep relationships light and easy at this time.

11 SUNDAY *Moon Age Day 4 Moon Sign Sagittarius*

Avoid making spur of the moment purchases today and keep a tight hold on your money. Part of the problem is that Christmas is just around the corner, which is always expensive. Another stumbling block is that you might make what you think is an excellent buy, only to find the same item cheaper elsewhere.

12 MONDAY *Moon Age Day 5 Moon Sign Capricorn*

Your social life is extremely important to you; in fact it is sometimes difficult to know where other aspects of your life stop and social interaction begins. You will be especially good at mixing business with pleasure across the next few days and you can do yourself no end of good by maintaining good relations with colleagues.

13 TUESDAY *Moon Age Day 6 Moon Sign Capricorn*

Today you exhibit masses of charm but at the same time display a powerful personality. People that matter could be noticing you around this time and the fact that you are so inclined to persevere will not be lost on them. You might not realise that you are under scrutiny but it is likely to be taking place all the same.

14 WEDNESDAY *Moon Age Day 7 Moon Sign Aquarius*

There might not be time to do everything you had planned today but whether this is the case or not you do need to be certain that what you do is undertaken properly and efficiently. It is far more important for the moment to achieve your objectives in a limited way and that way you begin to see light at the end of a very long tunnel.

15 THURSDAY   *Moon Age Day 8   Moon Sign Aquarius*

In your dealings with others you will probably show less self-control than would sometimes be the case. Sometimes you can be frank to the point of being rude and maybe a little more diplomacy would help. In particular, avoid getting on the wrong side of people who will soon be in a position to help you out.

16 FRIDAY   *Moon Age Day 9   Moon Sign Aquarius*

What sets today apart? Well it looks as though you will be extremely sensitive and quite easily brought to tears. This is probably not on your own account but in response to the problems of others. You can even feel bad about something that is happening at the other side of the world but fortunately such trends don't last long for the Archer.

17 SATURDAY   ☿   *Moon Age Day 10   Moon Sign Pisces*

With the weekend comes a desire to get things sorted out at home. If you are a DIY enthusiast you will now be tearing down walls, building new ones or redecorating. There is a strong spring-clean feeling about which, though odd for this time of year, will make you feel better and when you feel better you act more spontaneously.

18 SUNDAY   ☿   *Moon Age Day 11   Moon Sign Pisces*

All the love and devotion you can muster is now being heaped upon someone who is very special to you. Those little things that make all the difference come as second nature to you at the moment and making someone really happy is more or less what your life is about today. Try to smooth out disagreements at home.

19 MONDAY   ☿   *Moon Age Day 12   Moon Sign Aries*

You want to have things just so, especially at home. 'A place for everything and everything in its place' is hardly your usual adage but seems to be so under present planetary trends. This might surprise those with whom you live and can also be a cause of no small amusement.

20 TUESDAY ☿ *Moon Age Day 13 Moon Sign Aries*

When it comes to the needs of relatives and friends you will probably be quite outspoken today and you won't take kindly to seeing anyone used or put upon. The Archer now decides that it has the solutions to the world's problems and will set out to put things right. That's fine in principle but slightly more difficult in practice.

21 WEDNESDAY ☿ *Moon Age Day 14 Moon Sign Taurus*

As far as work is concerned difficult jobs are done in a moment, while impossible ones could take just a little while longer. There could hardly be a better set of planetary circumstances when it comes to getting on well in life, though don't expect these trends to be with you indefinitely because there are hiccups.

22 THURSDAY ☿ *Moon Age Day 15 Moon Sign Taurus*

With some effort on your part you can reach destinations that seemed barred to you only a week or two ago. The change is probably in the attitude of those around you, some of whom are now much more willing to let you have your way. Don't get involved in arguments that have nothing to do with you.

23 FRIDAY ☿ *Moon Age Day 16 Moon Sign Taurus*

With one eye on the past and the other on the future you are able to learn from what you did before and to modify your stance as required. There are likely to be financial gains coming along all the time, even if these are small in size. What really matters is that you can make progress towards longer-term objectives.

24 SATURDAY ☿ *Moon Age Day 17 Moon Sign Gemini*

Put your biggest plans on the back burner and get some rest for the next couple of days. It isn't as if anything in particular is going wrong, merely that you don't feel as much like competing as might usually be the case. Your mind can wander far and wide but if you have the choice your body will be staying close to home.

25 SUNDAY ☿ *Moon Age Day 18   Moon Sign Gemini*

A brief time of withdrawal is still evident, though the lunar low this month can be turned to your advantage if only because it gives you more thinking time. With less stress around you can see things clearer than has been the case and that means that when the Moon moves on you will come out fighting straight away.

26 MONDAY ☿ *Moon Age Day 19   Moon Sign Cancer*

The more you throw in your lot with others during this part of the week the greater are the rewards that can come your way. It is true that you have to pay full attention at the moment and that you probably won't have quite the level of personal success you would wish but there is a good chance you are achieving more than you think.

27 TUESDAY ☿ *Moon Age Day 20   Moon Sign Cancer*

Go slowly today – not because there is any lack of energy or potential success but simply because the Archer is inclined to rush its fences and to fall occasionally as a result. The more circumspect you manage to be, the better is the chance that things will go your way. This is a time of opportunity and one that brings fun too.

28 WEDNESDAY ☿ *Moon Age Day 21   Moon Sign Leo*

Not every area of your life is equally productive at this time so take care about what you take on just now. Personal annoyance comes in your case from chasing a dream miles along the road, only to find it disappearing before your eyes. It's better to play for certainties than to indulge in pipe dreams.

29 THURSDAY ☿ *Moon Age Day 22   Moon Sign Leo*

Don't put off until another time what you can quite easily achieve now. People around you will be offering all sorts of possible diversions but there are jobs that need finishing and that has to come first. If you put down your tools now it will be more difficult to pick them up later and you may go down in the estimation of loved ones.

30 FRIDAY ☿ *Moon Age Day 23* *Moon Sign Virgo*

There are a few challenges to be dealt with at work but it is likely you will take these in your stride and actually enjoy the cut and thrust of a fairly demanding interlude. In the main you should be on top form and more than willing to take on even more adventures once the demands of the working day are out of the way.

December 2018

1 SATURDAY ☿ *Moon Age Day 24 Moon Sign Virgo*

Increased happiness can come from a gradually increasing feeling that you are now running your own ship. Sagittarius does not like to feel that someone else is totally in charge and you hate to be beholden to anyone. Today should offer significant social possibilities, most likely in the company of friends rather than relatives.

2 SUNDAY ☿ *Moon Age Day 25 Moon Sign Libra*

Your mind and your actions will turn more in the direction of those you love today. Although you are likely to retain your ability to get things right first time if you are at work, there are needs and wants coming from your relatives that will take up more of your time generally. Splitting your day could be problematic, but possible all the same.

3 MONDAY ☿ *Moon Age Day 26 Moon Sign Libra*

Creature comforts will be of relatively little importance right now and you will be more or less ignoring any need for greater security or forward planning. On the contrary you tend to make up your mind instantly and to think much more about what is happening around you now. In more than one way you want to forge ahead.

4 TUESDAY ☿ *Moon Age Day 27 Moon Sign Scorpio*

All decisions are now being made instantly and without too much recourse to the opinions of others. It isn't that you are insensitive – merely that you are sure of your position and remain certain that what is good for you will help those around you. That might well be true but you will need to explain it to them.

5 WEDNESDAY ☿ *Moon Age Day 28 Moon Sign Scorpio*

Today should be slightly better when it comes to your poise and balance. You gradually begin to take others into consideration, not simply in your mind but verbally too. The strange thing is that once you do explain yourself practically everyone will fall in line. It's not what you do that counts but how you go about it.

6 THURSDAY ☿ *Moon Age Day 29 Moon Sign Scorpio*

There are possible gains to be made today on account of your quick thinking and your desire to act on impulse. This isn't always the case of course but for the moment people are willing to fall in line with your thinking and to support you. Too many rules and regulations are inclined to get on your nerves at times like this.

7 FRIDAY *Moon Age Day 0 Moon Sign Sagittarius*

There should be no difficulty in getting what you want from life on this particular Friday. Having the lunar high around makes for a good way to end the working week, even if it also makes you rather more impatient than you perhaps should be. Play the hand you are holding for all you are worth because fortune is smiling on you now.

8 SATURDAY *Moon Age Day 1 Moon Sign Sagittarius*

A surplus of physical energy is to be expected and perhaps for the first time this year you are now fully into Christmas mode. Indeed, if invitations for celebrations are not coming your way today you are likely to create them for yourself. Getting others to play along should be really easy because you are tremendously persuasive today.

9 SUNDAY *Moon Age Day 2 Moon Sign Capricorn*

You now have powerful feelings about certain issues and you won't let things ride. There are many conversations possible and some of these are vital if you want to maintain full control over your own destiny. Others may be reminding you that Christmas is coming but you won't worry about that for a while.

10 MONDAY   *Moon Age Day 3   Moon Sign Capricorn*

You should now be able to relax more in a professional sense. All the effort you put in previously is now likely to start paying dividends and you will be quite keen to make some major alteration with regard to the circumstances of your working life. At home you may be slightly annoyed by the strange behaviour of younger people.

11 TUESDAY   *Moon Age Day 4   Moon Sign Aquarius*

You are now at your best when you are firmly ensconced in tasks that take up most of your effort and attention. It is the fine details of life that matter the most under present planetary trends and that is slightly unusual for Sagittarius, which usually concerns itself with the bigger picture and broader trends. Don't be too picky with relatives.

12 WEDNESDAY   *Moon Age Day 5   Moon Sign Aquarius*

Expect friendly co-operation to be the order of the day when it comes to the professional side of your life, though this is less likely in a domestic or even a friendship sense. At the same time there are strong romantic signals in your chart so today turns out to be a mixed bag of both good and not-so-good trends.

13 THURSDAY   *Moon Age Day 6   Moon Sign Aquarius*

It may now be necessary to begin the reconstruction of certain parts of your life. There are gains to be made at the start of next year but the alterations necessary to get them will begin around now. Listen to the suggestions that are being made by colleagues and friends and don't dismiss a rather odd idea completely out of hand.

14 FRIDAY   *Moon Age Day 7   Moon Sign Pisces*

You know what you want to say today and won't have any difficulty at all getting your message across to others. The only slight fly in the ointment is that you could be rather too direct for some people and that could lead to arguments. There are times when you should be diplomatic and show sensitivity.

15 SATURDAY
Moon Age Day 8   Moon Sign Pisces

You may experience an increase in social engagements, which is of course to be expected so close to the festive season. All the same you want to concentrate on the practical side of life and won't take kindly to being shunted from pillar to post in order to please others. You can actually be quite cranky and awkward at the moment.

16 SUNDAY
Moon Age Day 9   Moon Sign Pisces

Some situations could seem irritating – even if the core of the problem is your own state of mind. You won't get everything you want simply by wishing it was so and extra effort will be necessary if you want to persuade others that you have all the answers. Get to grips with social demands before things get too hectic.

17 MONDAY
Moon Age Day 10   Moon Sign Aries

Laughter is truly the best tonic at the moment and you can really take the heat out of almost any situation with your cheerful and joking attitude to life. There are some slight financial gains on the way, even if these are only a realisation that you are slightly better off than you thought. Your confidence generally is beginning to grow.

18 TUESDAY
Moon Age Day 11   Moon Sign Aries

There are thoughts at the back of your mind that demand more of your attention today and you have what it takes to concentrate on things more than usual. Emotions could run high in the family and whether you realise it or not some of them are being jacked up by your own present attitude. Listen to younger people, especially today.

19 WEDNESDAY
Moon Age Day 12   Moon Sign Taurus

Just remember that even the Archer cannot please all of the people all of the time. There are likely to be a few people around now who will remain dissatisfied with whatever you do. Instead of concentrating on the awkward types you should be looking towards the multitude that think you are the bee's knees.

20 THURSDAY   *Moon Age Day 13   Moon Sign Taurus*

If there is some tension about today you can do a great deal to dissipate it merely by being your usual charming self. People love to have you around, partly because you are so good at entertaining them. You will be increasingly on show for the next few days, not just because of Christmas but also on account of changing planetary trends.

21 FRIDAY   *Moon Age Day 14   Moon Sign Gemini*

There may be a few complications today and it would be sensible to proceed fairly cautiously at first. The lunar low can make you feel as though you are not totally in charge of situations but this really isn't the case and everything should turn out fine in the end. All the same, it might be safest to seek out professional advice on occasion.

22 SATURDAY   *Moon Age Day 15   Moon Sign Gemini*

The ups and downs of everyday life will continue much as before but there is a sense that certain matters are changing now or are at least about to alter. Getting things working exactly as you would expect might not be all that easy at first and a good deal of application is needed if you want to feel fully in charge of your own destiny.

23 SUNDAY   *Moon Age Day 16   Moon Sign Cancer*

In the main you are a leader and not a follower. This tendency is much enhanced at present and you could easily fall out with those who try to insist that you follow any course of action that is not inspired from within yourself. You need to be in command and this is the fact that is likely to cause you a few upsets around now.

24 MONDAY   *Moon Age Day 17   Moon Sign Cancer*

Enjoy everything that Christmas Eve has to offer in the knowledge that almost everyone around you is happy and contented. That may also include you but under present trends there are bound to be things that seem too routine and inflexible. Curb your natural enthusiasm for upheaval, at least for Christmas.

25 TUESDAY
Moon Age Day 18   Moon Sign Leo

Christmas Day looks settled and there are trends about that indicate the possibility of meeting new people, so maybe you have decided to get out of the house at some stage. Whatever you decide to do you should be secure in the support and love of family members and especially your partner. Stand by for supersonic surprises.

26 WEDNESDAY
Moon Age Day 19   Moon Sign Leo

Now would be a good time for travel, even if you are only thinking in terms of short journeys to visit relatives or friends. You certainly will not want to stay at home throughout the whole Christmas period and will get bored unless you ring the changes in some way. You become more and more a party animal as the days progress.

27 THURSDAY
Moon Age Day 20   Moon Sign Virgo

Your ego is rather inflated, though there is nothing wrong about that as long as you use the trend constructively. There is just a slight possibility that you can upset others by being too abrupt or tactless, though this is something you can counter if you try.

28 FRIDAY
Moon Age Day 21   Moon Sign Virgo

From an emotional viewpoint you could be hanging on to issues and situations from the past that have little or nothing to do with your life at the moment. This is in sharp contrast to your more practical mind, which is proceeding without any interruption or delay. Two opposing attitudes at the same time might be somewhat confusing.

29 SATURDAY
Moon Age Day 22   Moon Sign Libra

Find the right people today – that is the most important advice whilst the Sun occupies its present position in your solar chart. It doesn't matter whether you need the chimney sweeping or if you want to organise a trip somewhere. There is always someone around who is an expert and you need to find that individual now.

30 SUNDAY
Moon Age Day 23   Moon Sign Libra

This is no time to gamble wildly on things turning out well simply because you want them to. What is required most at this particular time is better planning and a few trial runs. People generally should be fairly helpful but there will be one or two awkward people around who take more persuading than usual.

31 MONDAY
Moon Age Day 24   Moon Sign Libra

From a social point of view the world is definitely on your side today. Just be careful that you don't bite off more than you can chew. It might be best to keep the day generally quiet, so that by the evening you will be ready to party with the best of them. Sagittarius loves to party.

SAGITTARIUS:
2019 DIARY PAGES

SAGITTARIUS:
YOUR YEAR IN BRIEF

Although the year might start slowly, things will start to move as soon as you decide what your priorities should be. January and February offer you the chance to get to grips with pressing issues at work, whilst at the same time devoting some of your attention to changes you are making at home. Romance might take a back seat but not for long. If you have made some changes in your financial management, keep this up and spread your options across a number of different possibilities.

The start of March and April might seem busier by comparison and will offer plenty in the way of diversion and activity that looks likely to pay off well. Don't put off until later what you can do now because as the year advances you will get busier still. Romance looks especially good during these months and new relationships may start for some. Stretch yourself to take on new interests; a sport looks especially promising.

By the time May comes along you could be slightly confused by what has been happening around you but any negative trends quickly fall into the background. With the help of the planets you soon begin to formulate new plans and to get yourself involved in all sorts of possibilities that would have looked less than likely early in the year. Personal relationships will occupy a lot of your thinking, especially if you empathise with someone. June continues these trends but amplifies them.

In July and August you will be enjoying the best that the summer weather can offer and keen to get a move on with plans that might mean big changes in and around your home. You will also be travelling more, perhaps on unexpected journeys. People who live at a distance could be coming to see you and the high summer should be eventful and happy.

With the months of September and October comes a slight slowing of events and with this, your ambition. You might have to be content with second best at times, but you will still use all your effort, especially in monetary matters. Love shines brightly in your life and there are gains to be made from a change of job or a change of focus. People from the past may reappear in your life.

The last months of the year, November and December, should find you anxious to please, enthusiastic for new projects, and looking forward to a festive season that appears to have extra blessings this time around. Comfort and security are uppermost in your mind, and while you won't get everything you want you will have most of what you need and as a Sagittarius, you know that this is what really matters.

2019

1 TUESDAY
Moon Age Day 25   Moon Sign Scorpio

It's New Year's Day – and there's plenty to keep you occupied and busy. On top form, especially in a social sense, and with people gathering around you all the time this would be a good period to ask for something you really want. You may also be busy on the internet and engaged in sending and receiving text messages.

2 WEDNESDAY
Moon Age Day 26   Moon Sign Scorpio

Reputations seem to be at stake today, especially if someone is saying something about you that is definitely not true. You will want to defend yourself but there is a chance that if you do so with too much apparent conviction you might make things worse. It might be best to leave well enough alone for the moment.

3 THURSDAY
Moon Age Day 27   Moon Sign Sagittarius

With a somewhat quieter day in store you will be anxious to catch up on jobs at home but you won't relish your own company all day long. Later on you will probably choose to be out there amongst your friends, proving that you are the liveliest one of them all. In truth, though, you won't have to try very hard as everyone already knows it.

4 FRIDAY
Moon Age Day 28   Moon Sign Sagittarius

The more you learn about things, the greater is your capacity to put what you know to the test. There are some startling insights before you and maybe even one or two ridiculous coincidences. With a greater than usual sense of responsibility, you could be particularly protective of family members and old friends.

5 SATURDAY
Moon Age Day 0   Moon Sign Capricorn

Take care not to make too many promises today because, although many of them are gratifying, in the end you need to be careful about what you're committing to. Any get-rich-quick schemes should also definitely be avoided in favour of slow and steady progress. This might not be quite so appealing but is safer in the long run.

6 SUNDAY
Moon Age Day 1   Moon Sign Capricorn

The Archer is not generally known for its patience. You want everything available and you want it right now. This isn't going to be possible for today at least and you will have to set your sights somewhat lower than might usually be the case. Confidential conversations need to be kept that way so make sure you don't divulge any secrets.

7 MONDAY
Moon Age Day 2   Moon Sign Capricorn

Although it's only January you could already be feeling the need for a general spring clean. It isn't so much your possessions that need sorting out as your mind, though. You may be hanging on to thoughts and possibilities that no longer have any real relevance to your life and if so you will need to get things sorted out. A chat with a good friend might help.

8 TUESDAY
Moon Age Day 3   Moon Sign Aquarius

Trends indicate that some new responsibilities are in view for you – but that won't trouble you in the slightest. You should now be fully on form and quite willing to take on whatever life wants to throw at you. With new opportunities coming in all the time, today will seem like a period when you have just woken from a deep sleep. It's onward and upward!

9 WEDNESDAY
Moon Age Day 4   Moon Sign Aquarius

It isn't the mainstream of life that appeals to you today but rather its undercurrents. You want to know how everything works and will be doing all you can to discover what is 'really' going on. With your detective head on, you may get to the bottom of something that has been on your mind for a very long time now.

10 THURSDAY
Moon Age Day 5   Moon Sign Pisces

Standard responses simply to problematic issues won't be enough when it comes to family members. They want to know exactly what you have on your mind and won't be fudged. Maybe it's time to come clean and to tell the truth. The only problem is that there are times when the Archer struggles to know the real truth itself. Prepare for confusion to follow.

11 FRIDAY
Moon Age Day 6   Moon Sign Pisces

Trends move on and as things smooth over, the pace of your life now quickens as the normal responsibilities of work start to catch up with you. This will present a challenge rather than a problem. You know what you want from life right now and how to go about getting it. New contacts could come along at every turn this week.

12 SATURDAY
Moon Age Day 7   Moon Sign Pisces

As you are presently likely to be on the way up the ladder of achievement you might catch sight of one or two individuals who are definitely coming in the opposite direction. Show some care and concern because it is your true humanity that often sets you apart. The Archer is very charity-minded in all sorts of ways under present trends.

13 SUNDAY
Moon Age Day 8   Moon Sign Aries

Rules and regulations can definitely get on your nerves, especially if they interfere with your idea of a good Sunday. Fight shy of them today and do something different. Get out of the house with your partner or friends and just have a good time. No matter what you choose to do it's the fact that you undertake it with such panache that's important.

14 MONDAY
Moon Age Day 9   Moon Sign Aries

Although a new working week begins today the accent is definitely on the social side of your life. This either means that you are pushing your personality into your work, or that you are doing less in a practical sense in favour of pleasing yourself and mixing more freely. Someone special may also be on your mind for most of today.

15 TUESDAY *Moon Age Day 10   Moon Sign Taurus*

Social activities today should have an uplifting effect but where work is concerned avoid any temptation to pass the buck to others. You are quite capable of taking the rap yourself and there's every chance you will be more respected for doing so. The attitude of a particular friend could be rather puzzling later.

16 WEDNESDAY *Moon Age Day 11   Moon Sign Taurus*

Information could unaccountably go astray today, that is unless you are scrupulous in the way you organise yourself. Archers are not the tidiest people in the world and there is just the possibility that you are not paying full attention. A slight mistake now might mean hours putting things right at another time.

17 THURSDAY *Moon Age Day 12   Moon Sign Taurus*

A spirit of harmony should exist in group endeavours and there never was a better time to be getting on with just about anyone. You are slightly less sure of yourself on a one-to-one basis, especially if attention is coming your way that isn't welcome. People you don't see all that often could well be coming into your life again now.

18 FRIDAY *Moon Age Day 13   Moon Sign Gemini*

Social relationships look good but there may well be a part of you that really wants to curl up in a corner and be by yourself. This dichotomy often prevails in the life of Sagittarians. Mix and match is the best way forward. You can have more or less whatever you wish, just as long as you are sensible in the way you go about it.

19 SATURDAY *Moon Age Day 14   Moon Sign Gemini*

Box clever today and allow someone else to take some of the strain. The Moon has moved into your opposite zodiac sign, bringing that time of the month that is known as the lunar low. Attitude is the most important factor, together with being willing to slow down and take stock. Real activity will come later.

20 SUNDAY   *Moon Age Day 15   Moon Sign Cancer*

You should be doing everything you can right now to make life less complicated than it might otherwise be. Simplify everything you can, certainly at work you will need to be more organised and less stressed. If there's something you can't do, ask someone who knows better because they are sure to lend a hand.

21 MONDAY   *Moon Age Day 16   Moon Sign Cancer*

You could prove to be especially good in debates or in just getting your views across in a family discussion. Friends seem more than willing to do anything they can to please you and the romantic prospects for this Monday are also looking pretty good. Confidences need to be kept so don't divulge anyone's secrets.

22 TUESDAY   *Moon Age Day 17   Moon Sign Leo*

There could be some conflict behind the scenes today, even though everyone is smiling in a way that says things are fine. Use your intuition, which is usually good but especially strong at present. You may need to give some very special support to a younger family member who may be having problems now.

23 WEDNESDAY   *Moon Age Day 18   Moon Sign Leo*

Close emotional attachments are highlighted in your chart right now and this is the best time of the month to simply say 'I love you' to that very special person. Plan now to give someone a real treat at the weekend but don't say anything about it. Surprises are something you presently tend to be very good at springing.

24 THURSDAY   *Moon Age Day 19   Moon Sign Virgo*

It looks as though minor tasks and obligations are going to remind you of your limitations at the moment. Sagittarians have their ups and downs but most of them don't last for more than about ten minutes. If you are bored or stressed, simply find something different to do, especially in the evening.

25 FRIDAY
Moon Age Day 20   Moon Sign Virgo

Certain emotional matters could prove to be quite a bind today, though not if you make a conscious decision to vary your routines and to push for a fun sort of day. There are always going to be people around who want to lend you a hand and the Archer is never short of friends. Rely on them a little today.

26 SATURDAY
Moon Age Day 21   Moon Sign Libra

If you want some peace and quiet away from the cut and thrust of everyday life, this weekend should be able to offer it. Don't get bogged down with responsibilities that are not really yours and encourage others to make their own decisions. You can't live anyone's life for them today but you also need some time to live your own.

27 SUNDAY
Moon Age Day 22   Moon Sign Libra

Now you should find that you have the necessary personal freedom to pursue hopes and dreams that stand out in your mind. Something you have wanted to do for quite a while should soon become a reasonable objective, though probably not without the support of a few important people. Start setting out your stall today.

28 MONDAY
Moon Age Day 23   Moon Sign Scorpio

In a social sense it seems that you have a good attitude and you will be the centre of whatever is going on in your vicinity. You have it within you to raise the spirits of people who are down in the dumps and there is nothing more rewarding than that. Don't allow yourself to become involved in pointless family arguments today.

29 TUESDAY
Moon Age Day 24   Moon Sign Scorpio

Social events reveal that your communication skills are second to none this Tuesday but the time taken on them probably leaves little time to concentrate on practical situations. Accept this for what it is – you need some time off occasionally and can't keep planning and doing all the time. Today is for being the centre of attention and having fun.

30 WEDNESDAY *Moon Age Day 25*   *Moon Sign Sagittarius*

Now the Moon enters your own zodiac sign of Sagittarius, bringing with it that part of the month that is known as the lunar high. You are more or less bound to be on top form and should be up for any sort of excitement. People you really care about are definitely on your side at the moment and should find ways to prove their regard for you.

31 THURSDAY   *Moon Age Day 26*   *Moon Sign Sagittarius*

Your charming manner ensures that your popularity remains high and that you have what it takes to impress those important people. Socially speaking you are definitely on form and will want to be doing all you can to mix with as many different sorts of people as you possibly can.

February 2019

1 FRIDAY
Moon Age Day 27   Moon Sign Sagittarius

Things are still looking good as the weekend approaches. Finish the working week with a definite flourish and do what you can to get ahead in the business stakes. Good luck is likely to be on your side so you can afford to take the odd chance. Keep your gambling to a minimum though because luck only stretches so far.

2 SATURDAY
Moon Age Day 28   Moon Sign Capricorn

Utilise the stimulating mental environment that surrounds you right now. Go for your ideas in a big way and show other people just how adaptable and quick your mind actually is. It might be possible to make a little financial gain at the moment, but you will need to be very speedy in order to do so.

3 SUNDAY
Moon Age Day 29   Moon Sign Capricorn

It may prove essential to put a particular matter to bed before you start on anything new and grand. There is no point at all in mixing things up under present trends so be absolutely sure that one phase is over before another begins. Don't get too worried about apparent rules and regulations. Carry on anyway.

4 MONDAY
Moon Age Day 0   Moon Sign Aquarius

You are now totally in your element when you are making changes, especially if you are also able to travel. In a social sense you will be suited best to situations that allow you to be in contact with others on a moment-by-moment basis. Being on your own too much is unlikely to appeal to you very much under present trends.

5 TUESDAY
Moon Age Day 1   Moon Sign Aquarius

There could be a rather independent and even argumentative quality to your mood around now and this is something you will have to guard against if you need to co-operate with others. Weigh up what you have to gain by arguing versus what you can achieve if you share resources. The conclusion should be very clear.

6 WEDNESDAY
Moon Age Day 2   Moon Sign Aquarius

Make sure you don't become over obsessed with a certain issue. It's best for Sagittarians to spread their talents around and that's the way you should be handling things at the moment. People from the past could find their way into your life again, possibly with some startling revelations and results. Keep calm when at work.

7 THURSDAY
Moon Age Day 3   Moon Sign Pisces

It would be better to deal with work matters on your own now. The idea of anyone dogging your heels will be both unpleasant and distracting, but it is also necessary to achieve your objectives without upsetting anyone. Let that silver Sagittarian tongue and charm come to the fore and smooth things over. You don't need aggravation.

8 FRIDAY
Moon Age Day 4   Moon Sign Pisces

Trends indicate that today is ripe for new ideas, at least some of which have a bearing on your practical life. In the evening you might choose to seek out certain friends and you should also be feeling close to your family. Keep an eye on money and in particular what you are spending your money on.

9 SATURDAY
Moon Age Day 5   Moon Sign Aries

If it looks as though there is not enough in your life that you could call exciting or ambitious, it will be up to you to do something about it. Some of the help you need could come from your associations with others. Relationships should be not only happy today but could also prove to be practically useful and quite profitable too.

10 SUNDAY   *Moon Age Day 6   Moon Sign Aries*

The bright lights of the social world cheer you up no end, especially right now. If life is feeling rather dull, make sure that your free time is spent in company that you both know and like. In discussions with others you should want to take centre stage and impress those around you with your knowledge.

11 MONDAY   *Moon Age Day 7   Moon Sign Aries*

Intimate relationships are what make life interesting at this time. Do what you can to be supportive to your friends, and also let the one you love know how important they are to you. A little present, or a kind word could make all the difference. What you need most now is to offer reassurance to everyone.

12 TUESDAY   *Moon Age Day 8   Moon Sign Taurus*

For a number of reasons you now want to emphasise the practical side of life and have the right sort of mental ammunition to take on the job. There are a few outstanding issues that have to be addressed, even if to do so is quite hard and perhaps even a little depressing. You can get where you need to be, but it will take time right now.

13 WEDNESDAY   *Moon Age Day 9   Moon Sign Taurus*

A few small irritations surrounding debates of any sort should not be allowed to get in the way of general progress with your professional life. In the middle of this working week you are in the mood for adventure and should also find that trends bring you the opportunity to travel more than has been possible of late.

14 THURSDAY   *Moon Age Day 10   Moon Sign Gemini*

If you are setting out to obtain a particular objective, you will need to plan ahead and make sure that your strategy is the correct one. In amongst the hustle and bustle of life you sometimes need to take day out. As this is the time of the lunar low, it is as good a time as any, and better than most. Don't be disappointed by temporary failure.

15 FRIDAY   *Moon Age Day 11   Moon Sign Gemini*

This is likely to be another quiet day and one that offers you the chance to observe the general patterns that are taking place around you in every sphere of your life. Taking any sort of action is only sensible once you have first weighed up the pros and cons of situations. That is what days such as this allow and even encourage you to do.

16 SATURDAY   *Moon Age Day 12   Moon Sign Cancer*

Don't give way to excessive optimism now or you could find yourself coming unstuck. You would instead be better off to view things with a critical eye and not necessarily believe everything you either read or are told. The path to success is a little harder this weekend, but it's still well marked for many Sagittarians.

17 SUNDAY   *Moon Age Day 13   Moon Sign Cancer*

The accent today is on the domestic scene. That might not be too surprising on a Sunday and it is important to make the most of family ties. Stimulation comes from being able to make your own choices and perhaps from new hobbies of one sort or another. Keep abreast of news and current affairs if you can, as there is a small chance you could benefit from them.

18 MONDAY   *Moon Age Day 14   Moon Sign Leo*

This could be a day of reasonable gains in a financial sense, possibly because of decisions you made some time ago or maybe the generosity of a family member. You need to feel secure at home and that might mean thinking about some changes. Most Sagittarians will also now be going through a distinctly creative period.

19 TUESDAY   *Moon Age Day 15   Moon Sign Leo*

Intellectual exchanges are now your forte and – typical of your sign – you like to mix with as many different types of people as you possibly can. Don't be ruled by the past and instead push your mind forward as much as possible. Something you are saying stands a chance of being misconstrued so it's important to explain yourself.

20 WEDNESDAY *Moon Age Day 16   Moon Sign Virgo*

All things domestic appear to be highly fulfilling today and you are likely to be turning away from strictly professional matters at this stage of the week. You would now be more likely to allow others to take some of the strain whilst you enjoy some time to yourself. Confidence is everything when it comes to new hobbies.

21 THURSDAY *Moon Age Day 17   Moon Sign Virgo*

Don't expect to win everyone round to your point of view today because that simply is not going to happen. It's possible that you are seen as being more assertive than you intend to be and if this is the case it would be good to ease off at some stage and show what a great sense of humour you have. Not everyone knows you as well as they might.

22 FRIDAY *Moon Age Day 18   Moon Sign Libra*

Watch carefully the way you are dealing with others because there's a possibility that you are not quite as diplomatic as you might be. It's important to explain yourself fully and to come to terms with the needs of family members and your partner. There is a danger that you could be unintentionally a little caustic.

23 SATURDAY *Moon Age Day 19   Moon Sign Libra*

Certain tasks you have to undertake today could prove to be slightly stressful but if you keep smiling this tendency might pass you by. Friends should be particularly supportive at present and are likely to be offering you a chance to make some money. Have some fun in the evening.

24 SUNDAY *Moon Age Day 20   Moon Sign Scorpio*

A period of emotional ups and downs is indicated, and is something you probably cannot avoid today. Play things cool and don't become drawn into arguments that are not of your making. Someone you know well is in need of a little moral support and you should be in just the right position to offer it.

25 MONDAY *Moon Age Day 21   Moon Sign Scorpio*

Very little should steer you off course today and the planetary line-up looks much more promising. The new week brings the chance of more excitement than has been possible for the last few days. Family arrangements might have to be altered but you will almost certainly rise to any occasion.

26 TUESDAY *Moon Age Day 22   Moon Sign Sagittarius*

Put your best foot forward and make the very best of some extremely positive planetary happenings. The lunar high especially will improve your level of good luck and should afford you a greater chance to score some significant successes. In your present mood, you are now the sort of person everyone would wish to know.

27 WEDNESDAY *Moon Age Day 23   Moon Sign Sagittarius*

Your intuition is now likely to be very accurate and you seem to be able to see through all situations in an instant. This means you will make up your mind to a course of action quickly and you won't be easily diverted from any chosen path. Lady Luck remains on your side and may assist you to make good use of routine events or coincidences.

28 THURSDAY *Moon Age Day 24   Moon Sign Sagittarius*

It looks as though you maintain a high degree of confidence, although perhaps a little too much for your own good. Take situations one at a time and wait for more promising times before you take any irrevocable decisions. The quieter side of your personality could be the most rewarding just now, and creative activities could be good.

March

2019

1 FRIDAY
Moon Age Day 25   Moon Sign Capricorn

Material issues could lead to a few pitfalls today, so be especially careful, particularly with money. Stand up for friends who feel they are under attack because your presence in the situation can make all the difference. If you do argue at all today make sure that it is on behalf of others and not yourself.

2 SATURDAY
Moon Age Day 26   Moon Sign Capricorn

It would be best to keep your options open today and not to commit yourself to a specific course of action. Trends suggest that there are people around who are genuinely on your side and others who simply pretend to be. Telling the difference should not be all that difficult as your intuition is especially well honed at this time.

3 SUNDAY
Moon Age Day 27   Moon Sign Aquarius

It is possible that you will find yourself in conflict with your partner or a family member today and you should really withdraw from such situations if you can. Better by far to bite your tongue for the moment, especially since you might be wrong. Tomorrow is another day and you won't be so adamant by then.

4 MONDAY
Moon Age Day 28   Moon Sign Aquarius

Though commitments taken on at the moment are not based on the securest of foundations you are likely to do better with long-term plans. Stay away from disputes, especially at work because they are not of your making and you can't gain anything by being involved. Romance could blossom around now.

5 TUESDAY   *Moon Age Day 29   Moon Sign Aquarius*

Long-distance travel and any sort of intellectual exchange clearly appeal to you at this time. You want to seek out fresh fields and pastures new and that's exactly what your astrological chart suggests. Don't be sold short regarding anything that rightfully belongs to you and be willing to stick up for yourself.

6 WEDNESDAY   ☿   *Moon Age Day 0   Moon Sign Pisces*

You may be moving from strength to strength in terms of professional matters at the moment but will probably have to take a holiday from such thoughts today. If you can, make today your own and find ways to enjoy yourself in the company of people you really like and who fire your imagination.

7 THURSDAY   ☿   *Moon Age Day 1   Moon Sign Pisces*

It is possible you will feel yourself coming to the end of a specific chapter in your life and of course that means starting another. There might be a little nostalgia about but it's necessary to move on and Sagittarians don't dwell on anything for long, as a general rule. Be careful not to accidentally betray a confidence at this time.

8 FRIDAY   ☿   *Moon Age Day 2   Moon Sign Aries*

Today's news on the personal front is likely to put you into a very positive frame of mind. Concern for family members and even friends might be high but there is a danger that it could be a little misplaced. Instead of finding reasons to worry, look for positive and inspirational situations, which are all around you now.

9 SATURDAY   ☿   *Moon Age Day 3   Moon Sign Aries*

Look out for a beneficial period in terms of social commitments and the possibility of advancement in your career. People are still generally helpful but sorting out the wheat from the chaff is a prerequisite of today. Don't get bogged down with details that don't really matter and keep your mind on the task at hand.

10 SUNDAY ☿ *Moon Age Day 4 Moon Sign Taurus*

This could be a day during which you are looking back at the recent past and coming to terms with certain emotional issues. Do away with any regrets because they are really of no use to you at the moment. Some of the gains that are waiting in the wings could be significantly greater than you had been expecting.

11 MONDAY ☿ *Moon Age Day 5 Moon Sign Taurus*

Avoid people who sound too good to be true right now because it's an odds-on certainty that they are. Before you can get down to doing what you really want today there is a certain amount of dross to get out of the way. An early start would help and then you will be into the interesting stuff that much sooner.

12 TUESDAY ☿ *Moon Age Day 6 Moon Sign Taurus*

Stick around familiar places and faces if you can today because that is where you are going to feel most at ease. You won't be too happy to spread yourself too thinly, which is odd for the Archer but is happening now because of the position of the Moon. You might decide to visit someone you don't see too often.

13 WEDNESDAY ☿ *Moon Age Day 7 Moon Sign Gemini*

You might tend to think that the grass is greener on the other side of the fence today, mainly because of the negative position of the Moon. Convince yourself that this isn't the case and show some patience for the next couple of days. This would not a good time to spend money on any item you don't really need.

14 THURSDAY ☿ *Moon Age Day 8 Moon Sign Gemini*

When it comes to being decisive, which is usually second nature to you, you really struggle to be so at the moment. Better by far to allow others to make some of the running and to watch and wait for a while. At least your love life is likely to be going well and you could even receive some very special compliments around now.

15 FRIDAY ☿ *Moon Age Day 9   Moon Sign Cancer*

Looking after your health is important under present trends and it's important that you don't put too much pressure on yourself, especially when it comes to unnecessary stress. Be willing to look someone in the eye and tell them they are wrong, even if it's a superior. They won't respect you any less for speaking your mind.

16 SATURDAY ☿ *Moon Age Day 10   Moon Sign Cancer*

In professional matters, you should avoid hasty actions and think carefully before you make any move. Personally speaking, life should be somewhat easier and offer you the chance to make an important conquest. Single Archers especially can expect an eventful day.

17 SUNDAY ☿ *Moon Age Day 11   Moon Sign Cancer*

Keep a lookout today for people you haven't seen for a while. Their presence in your life now could prove to be quite fortuitous. Confronting issues from the past is a must at the moment because you are now in a position to straighten them out in your mind. Something you have been worrying about is likely to disappear.

18 MONDAY ☿ *Moon Age Day 12   Moon Sign Leo*

There is a tendency for you to have to put things right that should have been done and finished previously. In some instances, it won't be your fault, but there doesn't appear to be any choice. Even when you know that others have been careless or slipshod, it will be up to you to straighten things out. It isn't fair, but that's life.

19 TUESDAY ☿ *Moon Age Day 13   Moon Sign Leo*

There are many ingenious ideas coming into your head now. Although there probably isn't too much you can do about them at the moment, you do have your thinking head on today and could easily spend some time planning. New hobbies or interests that surface again in your life are noticeable now.

20 WEDNESDAY ☿ *Moon Age Day 14 Moon Sign Virgo*

Joint finances are one area of life that you could feel the need to address today. This won't interest you very much, but such things have to be done. You can sugar the pill by giving yourself one very enjoyable task for every one that doesn't please you so much.

21 THURSDAY ☿ *Moon Age Day 15 Moon Sign Virgo*

The continuing trend of better finances is partly due to planetary influence but also responds to the very responsible attitude you have been taking of late. Continue this process by dealing with family money. Not everyone is going to be pleased with what you have to say, but carry on anyway.

22 FRIDAY ☿ *Moon Age Day 16 Moon Sign Libra*

Family life appeals to you today and you should be doing all you can to sort out little problems at home that have been building up for a few days. You should make the time to get to know younger family members better, as they mature so quickly. Friends will be welcome, but they will have to come to you.

23 SATURDAY ☿ *Moon Age Day 17 Moon Sign Libra*

Your ability to get others on-side is strong and you need to make the most of it. Here, the strength of your personality comes to the fore. You might think that you fail to make the sort of impression that really counts, but before today is out you are likely to discover that this isn't the case at all.

24 SUNDAY ☿ *Moon Age Day 18 Moon Sign Scorpio*

Information coming your way from friends simply has to be listened to now. Although you might have a few doubts about the integrity of one specific individual, they are more likely to come good than to let you down. It's all a matter of trust, and you don't really lack that as a rule.

25 MONDAY ☿ *Moon Age Day 19 Moon Sign Scorpio*

The start of the week should be zippy and interesting. You tend to mix now with those people who have a similar attitude to life but that doesn't mean you can't get to know newcomers. Concentrate on the matter at hand in business, but don't rule out the possibility of good social trends later.

26 TUESDAY ☿ *Moon Age Day 20 Moon Sign Sagittarius*

What really should strike home today is how lucky you are. There are strong indications that you are now taking plans from the past and running with them. You can make the most of the assistance on offer as well as putting your own personal slant on life. In any situation it is worth committing yourself fully.

27 WEDNESDAY ☿ *Moon Age Day 21 Moon Sign Sagittarius*

The signal is up to make the very most of all situations. In a confident mood, you have what it takes to put in that extra bit of effort that can make all the difference to any outcome. When it comes to dealing with a habit or situation you hate, the ball is definitely in your court. You will be committed to success on all fronts.

28 THURSDAY ☿ *Moon Age Day 22 Moon Sign Capricorn*

The emphasis shifts from practical matters to partnerships, though not necessarily personal ones. If you are involved with someone in business, now is the time to redraw the guidelines you both follow. This is going to take serious discussion, which isn't as easy as it sounds now that you are in a flippant frame of mind.

29 FRIDAY *Moon Age Day 23 Moon Sign Capricorn*

Some of your plans could be waylaid today, most likely by circumstances rather than by other people. If you suddenly feel you need some excitement in your life, this is the time to go out and look for it. With good creative abilities, you could do much to improve your living surroundings and circumstances now.

30 SATURDAY   *Moon Age Day 24   Moon Sign Capricorn*

Your sense of adventure steps up a degree, making you more willing to take physical chances and keener than ever to get away. It is very easy to become bored with routines, while holiday brochures beckon. If it is impossible to travel now, you can at least plan a journey for later.

31 SUNDAY   *Moon Age Day 25   Moon Sign Aquarius*

The impulse for personal freedom is now extremely strong. It is very difficult to resist simply dropping everything and taking a trip. This restless streak is something you will have to fight hard against on a number of occasions at the moment. Simply breaking usual routines may help matters.

April

2019

1 MONDAY
Moon Age Day 26   Moon Sign Aquarius

Today might not prove to be the best day of the month when it comes to your love life. Either you are in a strange frame of mind or your partner is. For at least some of the time today it would be best to stick with friends because you will be getting on better with them in a general sense.

2 TUESDAY
Moon Age Day 27   Moon Sign Pisces

Your sense of humour is extremely important at this stage of the week. If those around you see that you are able to laugh at yourself they will think all the more of you. The winning ways of the Archer are now never far from the surface and you shine when in any sort of company, professional or social.

3 WEDNESDAY
Moon Age Day 28   Moon Sign Pisces

Once again you need to realise that this is not the best time of the month to think about going it alone. You would be far better off co-operating with others today, especially when it comes to social arrangements. Review past events in order to think up ways of increasing your earning power in the future.

4 THURSDAY
Moon Age Day 29   Moon Sign Pisces

There could be some rather sudden tensions arising in your life and you will be doing everything you can to avoid these. They are likely to be caused by the attitudes and opinions of others and the best thing to do is to simply ignore them. Stick with friends you know well and especially people who are not cynical or critical.

5 FRIDAY
Moon Age Day 0   Moon Sign Aries

There could be an element of luck involved in any career moves that come round about now. Nevertheless most of what is happening is down to your own effort across a considerable period of time. Don't be too quick to believe everything you are told, especially by sales people who might have a vested interest in soft-soap.

6 SATURDAY
Moon Age Day 1   Moon Sign Aries

A financial matter could just spoil your otherwise good mood to start the weekend. It's possible that you have trusted someone with money and might feel a little let down by their actions. Life can prove demanding on your pocket but there are things you can do now that are enjoyable but which don't cost a penny.

7 SUNDAY
Moon Age Day 2   Moon Sign Taurus

Those things that are not succeeding in the outside world should be ignored for the moment in favour of tackling what you know is working well for you. Don't get involved in get-rich-quick schemes because they rarely work out. Rock solid investments work best for you now, both in terms of time and money.

8 MONDAY
Moon Age Day 3   Moon Sign Taurus

There could be slight problems with cash and you would do best to keep your money firmly locked into your purse or wallet. There's a time for spending and a period when it is best to save and you are right in the middle of the latter now. Stick to something that's cheap, perhaps a ride out to somewhere beautiful?

9 TUESDAY
Moon Age Day 4   Moon Sign Gemini

Certain unique planetary positions make this one of the best days of the month for starting new projects. With plenty of enthusiasm and the greatest determination possible to succeed, what is likely to stand in your way? Avoid unnecessary routines and stick to the task in hand.

10 WEDNESDAY   *Moon Age Day 5   Moon Sign Gemini*

Certain situations may not work out well for you today and although you barely noticed that presence of the lunar low yesterday, it is definitely in operation now. Sit back and watch the spectacle of life for a day or two, even though your usual position is right up there on the stage in amongst the action.

11 THURSDAY   *Moon Age Day 6   Moon Sign Gemini*

Now is a time to make strides forward with regard to your long-term ambitions, especially later in the day. There are gains to be made from simply talking to the right people and ideas that you have had for some time are now likely to work out well. Family members may bring joy into your life and make you very proud of them.

12 FRIDAY   *Moon Age Day 7   Moon Sign Cancer*

You could find yourself involved in a very competitive situation that has something to do with money and it would definitely be best not to jump in with both feet as you are sometimes inclined to do. A little caution now can pay handsomely in the end because rushing in where angels fear to tread isn't always wise.

13 SATURDAY   *Moon Age Day 8   Moon Sign Cancer*

The green light is on and this is a day for positive and decisive action. Getting onside with the best players in life is a piece of cake and you know what you want instinctively. Everyone is likely to lend a hand but what matters most at present is your natural good luck.

14 SUNDAY   *Moon Age Day 9   Moon Sign Leo*

You may decide to opt for a total change of scenery today and if so you will need to relinquish control of something, at least temporarily. You have what it takes to not only make fun for yourself but for a host of other people too. Concentrate on putting right something that is proving to be an irritation in your love life.

15 MONDAY   *Moon Age Day 10   Moon Sign Leo*

Though you are fond of independence it might not be possible today to please yourself all the time. You live in a world filled with other people, most of whom have a definite point of view of their own. Where your world meets that of others you have little choice but to look for compromises.

16 TUESDAY   *Moon Age Day 11   Moon Sign Virgo*

This would be a very good time for important discussions and for making up your mind to get on with situations that have been waiting around for some time. You should discover that there is a great deal of help around when you need it the most and this comes from well-meaning friends.

17 WEDNESDAY   *Moon Age Day 12   Moon Sign Virgo*

In a professional sense things should now be going with a swing. If there isn't quite as much time to spend with your loved ones as you would wish you can take heart because that situation is likely to be remedied later in the week. Someone who is above you in the pecking order could be especially useful today.

18 THURSDAY   *Moon Age Day 13   Moon Sign Libra*

Your ideas and views could be challenged in some way today and it's important that you keep your cool and that you don't react too harshly to any situation. There ought to be more time to spend at home as the working week moves on and you will also be more romantic by inclination quite soon.

19 FRIDAY   *Moon Age Day 14   Moon Sign Libra*

This is a much better time than you have experienced all week in which to sit back and look at your life in a positive way. Don't try to get too much done in a concrete sense, though you might decide to do a little gardening or to have a short trip out to somewhere you consider to be very beautiful.

20 SATURDAY   *Moon Age Day 15   Moon Sign Scorpio*

Be on the lookout for newcomers who are likely to be entering your social life around this time. Although you have many acquaintances it looks as though new and long-lasting friends could be on the way. One or two of them can have a tremendous part to play in your life as it unfolds in the weeks and months ahead.

21 SUNDAY   *Moon Age Day 16   Moon Sign Scorpio*

This is a good time for building upon recent successes. If you are at work, you can consolidate your achievements and convince almost anyone that you know what you are talking about and should be trusted with more responsibility. Your social life ought to be working out well too, with a number of important invitations on the way.

22 MONDAY   *Moon Age Day 17   Moon Sign Sagittarius*

Now the decks are really cleared for action and it looks as though you have everything you need to get ahead. Any negative thoughts from the last couple of days will disappear like the morning mist, leaving you in the right frame of mind to really make progress. It seems like the whole world loves you now.

23 TUESDAY   *Moon Age Day 18   Moon Sign Sagittarius*

Look ahead to new beginnings in social matters. As a willing team member you get on well with just about everyone and can easily modify your own stance to suit whatever is going on around you. Private conversations can bring some especially exciting news, perhaps regarding future travel plans.

24 WEDNESDAY   *Moon Age Day 19   Moon Sign Capricorn*

Someone in your daily life is likely to be influencing the way you are thinking in the middle of this week. Although you are still determined enough to make up your mind about most things, words of wisdom will stay in your mind and could cause you to modify a course of action that might be a little too radical.

25 THURSDAY   *Moon Age Day 20   Moon Sign Capricorn*

You really will be in a mood to do your own thing today and won't take no for an answer once you have made up your mind about anything specific. If you sense that your ideas might be somewhat too radical for someone close to you, that fact could act as a red light. Maybe this will be no bad thing.

26 FRIDAY   *Moon Age Day 21   Moon Sign Capricorn*

The odd little personal problem might be on your mind and could possibly get in the way of smooth progress at work. You will need to focus at present and to have the confidence that you are dealing with things as positively as you can. Make sure you finish one task before starting on another just at the moment.

27 SATURDAY   *Moon Age Day 22   Moon Sign Aquarius*

This is likely to be an enjoyable day for you and it is possible to make the most of little opportunities that come your way. Generally speaking these will once again be more social than professional in nature. It is likely that people you see rarely might reappear in your life, either physically, by phone or on social media.

28 SUNDAY   *Moon Age Day 23   Moon Sign Aquarius*

This might be the best time of the month during which to reorganise your personal life in some way. Put your mind to work and take care of any details that you know need sorting out. Self-discipline ought to come easy and you are certainly not afraid of change.

29 MONDAY   *Moon Age Day 24   Moon Sign Pisces*

On a mundane level this would be a good day to focus specifically on your work and on the longer-term future. Career issues may now be becoming the most important ones but they are not exclusive. Later in the day there should be plenty of time to think about having fun, which is also very important at the moment.

30 TUESDAY

Moon Age Day 25   Moon Sign Pisces

There are obstacles to be overcome today though your real focus is likely to be on intimate issues. Now is the time to come to some sort of agreement with your partner or sweetheart and to also look very sympathetically on the way family members are thinking or acting. You can be especially understanding now.

May 2019

1 WEDNESDAY
Moon Age Day 26   Moon Sign Pisces

This is a day during which you need to focus on the practical side of life. You have to roll up your sleeves and to get stuck in, alongside others who clearly have your best interests at heart as well as their own. A low-key battle you have been fighting for some time could well be won around now.

2 THURSDAY
Moon Age Day 27   Moon Sign Aries

It is easy for you to attend to several different jobs at the same time today and still manage to do them all justice. That's not especially unusual for the Archer, though you do sometimes push yourself a little too hard. It also seems likely that you may get the opportunity to take some sort of interesting break.

3 FRIDAY
Moon Age Day 28   Moon Sign Aries

Personal concerns and domestic duties seem to be a major priority right now. It is possible that they will distract you from obligations elsewhere but as long as you make the necessary apologies you can deal with these later. What really matters today is not rushing things or overcrowding your schedule.

4 SATURDAY
Moon Age Day 0   Moon Sign Taurus

Social and teamwork efforts work best for you now and with less pressure on you in other areas of life than yesterday, things should go better. You are fairly sure what you want from life and will have a good idea about how to move forward. Don't be too quick to agree to something that is going to mean a great deal of work for no reward at all.

5 SUNDAY
Moon Age Day 1   Moon Sign Taurus

This may be a good time to assess how well certain plans are maturing. If they aren't moving at all, now is the period to think up new strategies. You are clearing the decks for action in a number of different ways though your attention is focused on the medium and long-term and not on the next few days.

6 MONDAY
Moon Age Day 2   Moon Sign Taurus

You are more ambitious at the start of this week than was probably the case for the last six or seven days. It is unlikely that you would be easily distracted from taking a course of action you know to be right, though you might modify your plans in the light of sound advice coming in from elsewhere.

7 TUESDAY
Moon Age Day 3   Moon Sign Gemini

Slacken the pace now and be willing to watch and wait. You can have a really good day, despite the lunar low, if you simply settle for what is on offer. It is possible you will be slightly quieter than usual and this could surprise a few people but in the main you are feeling pretty optimistic, though happy to wait a while.

8 WEDNESDAY
Moon Age Day 4   Moon Sign Gemini

Hold back on making any major decisions, if only for today. You really don't have all the details and in any case the support you need probably isn't in place. Last of all, your judgement isn't good whilst the lunar low is around. By the time tomorrow dawns you should be feeling a good deal better about most things.

9 THURSDAY
Moon Age Day 5   Moon Sign Cancer

If there are still any minor obstacles around you tend to be dealing with them quickly and efficiently. You will need to get your skates on today if you are going to get something done ahead of the competition but you think and act quickly so your ultimate success is really not in doubt.

10 FRIDAY
Moon Age Day 6   Moon Sign Cancer

Whilst your personal and emotional life ought to be singing now, the same cannot be said for family attachments, which look strained. It probably isn't your fault and it's clear that you will require a great deal of patience to get to the root of the problem. However, it will be worthwhile in the end and it's clear that your attitude is much appreciated.

11 SATURDAY
Moon Age Day 7   Moon Sign Leo

Get a complete change of scene if you can this weekend and let people know that you are going travelling because you will want some company. The Archer is not usually a solo player and especially not right now. Exciting new social developments are in the pipeline so it's worthwhile keeping your eyes open for them.

12 SUNDAY
Moon Age Day 8   Moon Sign Leo

Your ability to communicate is your strongest asset now, no matter what sphere of your life is involved. Don't keep quiet when you know it is necessary to speak out and be willing to act in a moment to protect your own interests. There is less awkwardness around at home but you still have to monitor the situation.

13 MONDAY
Moon Age Day 9   Moon Sign Virgo

Today could be make or break in a particular situation. You are liable to find a few people difficult to deal with but you are now equipped to take such matters in your stride. When you have to take decisions, keep everyone informed but do what you think is right in the end.

14 TUESDAY
Moon Age Day 10   Moon Sign Virgo

Personal relationships can sometimes seem to be more trouble than they are worth and that could certainly be the case at the moment. The fact is that your partner could be having a hard time and you will be on the receiving end of their stress. Be patient because things will settle down very quickly indeed.

15 WEDNESDAY   *Moon Age Day 11   Moon Sign Libra*

You seem to have plenty of charisma at the moment and will be approaching life pretty much as would be expected of a Sagittarian. Plans for travel are likely to be moving ahead and if you are seeking advancement at work, but not succeeding, now is the time to take your courage in your own hands and ask.

16 THURSDAY   *Moon Age Day 12   Moon Sign Libra*

Professional matters could prove to be a test of your patience, both today and tomorrow. Ring the changes when you can and avoid getting too involved in situations you know cannot be easily resolved. You will be more temperamentally suited to dealing with these later in the week.

17 FRIDAY   *Moon Age Day 13   Moon Sign Scorpio*

You should find yourself in the middle of a very active period socially now and there is plenty you can do to help yourself at this time. With lots of energy and a determination to see matters through to a satisfactory conclusion, you are able to address situations that looked quite daunting a few days ago.

18 SATURDAY   *Moon Age Day 14   Moon Sign Scorpio*

Trends suggest that you will be keeping in contact with people you know, and possibly also making some new friends this weekend. Educational matters look likely to go well, which is good news if you are studying, and there are likely to be romantic overtures of some sort, one or two of which could be especially surprising.

19 SUNDAY   *Moon Age Day 15   Moon Sign Scorpio*

There are likely to be ups and downs to be dealt with today. In particular, you should avoid falling out with your partner or sweetheart and also offer your friends the support they need. By tomorrow the oppressive trends in your chart will be over and you should begin to move forward with significant speed.

20 MONDAY   *Moon Age Day 16   Moon Sign Sagittarius*

This is definitely the best time of the month to put new ideas to the test. There's everything to play for and many situations that automatically work out the way you would wish. Routines are for the birds now because all you really want to do is to please yourself and to break down barriers as often as you can.

21 TUESDAY   *Moon Age Day 17   Moon Sign Sagittarius*

A bit of luck is marked in your chart today and it could crop up almost anywhere. You may feel the need to be the centre of attention and so will be more or less on duty all day long. In one way or another you will get noticed and since the lunar high supports you it's generally for the very best of reasons today.

22 WEDNESDAY   *Moon Age Day 18   Moon Sign Capricorn*

There are likely to be some disagreements, even if you are not the one creating them or even directly involved. Surprisingly for the Archer you can be the world's best diplomat today but you will need to be just a little careful all the same. It might be best to stay away from warring parties altogether.

23 THURSDAY   *Moon Age Day 19   Moon Sign Capricorn*

Problems and obstacles can be quite easily overcome, with a combination of common sense and intuition, especially as the behaviour of others in almost any given circumstance is likely to be very transparent. You should be able to contribute to the success presently being enjoyed by one or two family members.

24 FRIDAY   *Moon Age Day 20   Moon Sign Aquarius*

Someone may challenge you in a professional sense but you have broad shoulders at the moment and can deal with this sort of situation easily enough. Not everything goes your way right now but when it matters the most you have all the energy and determination to get you to the winning post.

25 SATURDAY   *Moon Age Day 21   Moon Sign Aquarius*

If you stay in close contact with others now you should be easily able to understand how their minds are working. This sort of deep intuition is important to your zodiac sign but not always present and it can be somewhat uncomfortable now because your empathy is so complete. Remember that you have your own life to live too.

26 SUNDAY   *Moon Age Day 22   Moon Sign Aquarius*

Today's planetary influences could incline you to be rather suspicious of the motives of other people and that can make for a rather uncomfortable day in some respects. It would be better to fight against this instinct and instead give others the benefit of the doubt, while trusting your own common sense. Better astrological trends are on the way.

27 MONDAY   *Moon Age Day 23   Moon Sign Pisces*

A big boost to your spirits may come courtesy of the changing position of the Moon in your solar chart. There is a good chance that you will feel very well disposed towards a particular friend or loved one and it is likely that your company is being avidly sought for social events of all kinds.

28 TUESDAY   *Moon Age Day 24   Moon Sign Pisces*

You may now be throwing all your energy into fulfilling some of your ambitions, especially in a professional and practical sense. There should be time for simple enjoyment later in the day, which will be welcome because it is important that you don't spend all day concentrating. Relaxation is vital by the time the evening comes along.

29 WEDNESDAY   *Moon Age Day 25   Moon Sign Aries*

This is a wonderful time to be with others and to enjoy the positive trends that are presently surrounding you. You can be more or less certain to give a good impression and your popularity is likely to be high. If there is something you want but you have been afraid to ask for it, this would be the best time to have a go.

30 THURSDAY   *Moon Age Day 26   Moon Sign Aries*

You encounter the new and the unusual in almost anything you undertake at the moment and will be quite pleased to take on something you would usually find unrealistic. Don't be held back by what you see as your limitations – believe yourself to be capable of anything. You won't be, but it's a start.

31 FRIDAY   *Moon Age Day 27   Moon Sign Aries*

Current trends seem to be geared towards personal gain and although this won't have so far been the best month you have ever known in a financial sense, things may improve a little now. Perhaps you will discover that you are better off than you expected or it could be that some surprise gains are on the way.

2019

1 SATURDAY
Moon Age Day 28   Moon Sign Taurus

The planetary focus at the beginning of a new month is definitely on teamwork. Friends should be willing to co-operate with you and offer you incentives to push harder, both at work and socially. With routines out of the window you are quite happy to take a chance and to make significant gains as a result.

2 SUNDAY
Moon Age Day 29   Moon Sign Taurus

Travel and intellectual matters are highlighted in your chart. You should be enjoying a little self-confidence at a time when it really matters. This Sunday should be a time of meetings and co-operation, sometimes with people you hardly knew before. New friendships could be the very positive result.

3 MONDAY
Moon Age Day 0   Moon Sign Gemini

This would not be a sensible time for struggling against the odds. On the contrary, if you are willing to sit and wait, everyone you want will come your way sooner or later. Of course this isn't an attitude that typifies Sagittarius but now the lunar low is around there isn't much point in knocking your head against a wall.

4 TUESDAY
Moon Age Day 1   Moon Sign Gemini

Some sort of setback is liable to take the wind out of your sails at some stage today. This is bound to be a fairly low-key period and as long as you don't try to carry on in the same old way, all should be well. Even the Archer needs a break now and again. Take comfort from the fact that good times lie ahead.

5 WEDNESDAY   *Moon Age Day 2   Moon Sign Cancer*

Your love life and romantic matters should now improve. It should be easy to keep your partner happy, or to set up an interesting date if you don't have a partner at the moment. Finding the right words to sweep someone off their feet is rarely difficult for you but today it's child's play.

6 THURSDAY   *Moon Age Day 3   Moon Sign Cancer*

You are now speeding ahead and accomplishing a great deal on the way. With plenty of zest and the ability to influence others, you may decide to push towards an objective you didn't think you would reach for some weeks or months. Pull out all the stops because good fortune is on your side right now.

7 FRIDAY   *Moon Age Day 4   Moon Sign Leo*

Patience will be required in any really trying situation to do with love at the moment. Don't expect sweetness and light coming from everyone because it just isn't going to be forthcoming at present. There's no point in being depressed about this, and in any case you have the power now to turn almost any situation around.

8 SATURDAY   *Moon Age Day 5   Moon Sign Leo*

You may wish to capitalise on a little good fortune that is now coming your way. It's possible you will want to make improvements at home and domestic matters are certainly likely to be on your mind throughout much of this weekend. Get into the swing of some alterations that are taking place at home.

9 SUNDAY   *Moon Age Day 6   Moon Sign Virgo*

There is likely to be considerable tension around you that is brought about by simple irritations. Shrug it off as best you can and concentrate on those things that you definitely know are going your way. Slow and steady wins any personal race and you will take kindly to some favours from friends.

10 MONDAY
Moon Age Day 7   Moon Sign Virgo

Decision-making should be suspended for today, but only because you have other things to do and won't want to sit around looking at the pros and cons of anything. Get as far away from ordinary life as you can and treat yourself to a dose of make believe, preferably in the company of someone you really care for.

11 TUESDAY
Moon Age Day 8   Moon Sign Virgo

Involvements with close friends and peers are very important today and you will be doing your best to impress people at every turn. Your desire to be friendly to one and all is noteworthy and you won't go short of the sort of attention that could turn almost anyone's head, but not that of a Sagittarian.

12 WEDNESDAY
Moon Age Day 9   Moon Sign Libra

Time spent alone should be a great boon today because although yours is the most gregarious of all the zodiac signs you still need time alone now and again. A little time set aside to think could mean that you come out on Thursday fighting like a tiger and with some fresh and interesting ideas to try.

13 THURSDAY
Moon Age Day 10   Moon Sign Libra

Financial matters show great promise of gain and there isn't much doubt about your ability to succeed at work around now. If you are between positions at the moment this is your time to concentrate all those efforts. Someone, somewhere, can't do without your unique talents. You just have to find out who they are.

14 FRIDAY
Moon Age Day 11   Moon Sign Scorpio

Romantic matters look settled and interesting now and you get the most pleasure from this area of life at the end of this working week. Not only are you saying all the right things but also some very welcome compliments may come back in your direction. Avoid spending money when it isn't necessary to do so.

15 SATURDAY *Moon Age Day 12   Moon Sign Scorpio*

This looks like being a socially beneficial period so prepare for a Saturday during which the practical side of life takes a back seat. Today it's important to enjoy yourself and to help others do the same. Life can be all smiles but it is important not to leave anyone out if you can avoid doing so.

16 SUNDAY *Moon Age Day 13   Moon Sign Sagittarius*

Opportunities are almost certain to present themselves today and this is certainly the best time of the month to put your capabilities on display. The world is on your side and listening very carefully to all you have to say. There are no rehearsals necessary at the moment and today will bring more breaks.

17 MONDAY *Moon Age Day 14   Moon Sign Sagittarius*

On a winning streak today, there isn't much that's beyond your power to control. Don't be bashful and remember that all eyes are on you. The entertainer is on display and that gives you the chance to star in any role you create for yourself. Life is certainly a ball for Archers who take the initiative now.

18 TUESDAY *Moon Age Day 15   Moon Sign Capricorn*

You are entering what is likely to be a reasonably good financial period, aided as you are by the present planetary line up. Joint business matters are likely to go well and you will find it quite possible to come to mutual agreements with others. However, you may experience a few small problems with younger family members.

19 WEDNESDAY *Moon Age Day 16   Moon Sign Capricorn*

Today should put you in the picture regarding a specific objective, probably one that is of a personal nature. Your imagination might not be quite what you need it to be and as a result you will have some boring moments to go through. If time hangs heavy on your hands, seek out a friend in the evening.

20 THURSDAY   *Moon Age Day 17   Moon Sign Capricorn*

You might be having difficulties with a friend or acquaintance at the moment and if so you will be once again more inclined to turn inward towards your partner or family members. The attitude of colleagues needs some thinking about but don't argue with them openly because that won't achieve anything.

21 FRIDAY   *Moon Age Day 18   Moon Sign Aquarius*

There are social bonuses to be had at present. Others will discover just how charming you can be and the best qualities of the Archer are now shining through. You are likely to be looking for entertainment and will gain as a result of your ability to lead the field when it comes to having a good time.

22 SATURDAY   *Moon Age Day 19   Moon Sign Aquarius*

This can be a time of intuitive awareness and a period during which you can easily assess the way others are likely to be thinking and acting. Although there are some delays to be dealt with at the moment, when it comes to getting others to do your bidding you have rarely been more successful.

23 SUNDAY   *Moon Age Day 20   Moon Sign Pisces*

This is a time during which you can reach out socially, probably in directions you hadn't really considered before. The attitude of some relatives is rather puzzling and you should certainly have more success with friends than family members. What could really irritate you at the moment are arrogant people, who you would be well advised to ignore.

24 MONDAY   *Moon Age Day 21   Moon Sign Pisces*

Career matters are on a roll at the start of this working week and you can gain a great deal by simply being in the right place at the right time. In a professional sense you may be comparing notes with colleagues and will be in a good frame of mind to co-operate right across the board.

25 TUESDAY *Moon Age Day 22 Moon Sign Pisces*

You might be somewhat too impulsive for your own good today and that means you must avoid taking decisions that will have a bearing on your life for weeks or months to come. Don't sign documents now unless you have no choice but if you must, make sure you read the small print as carefully as possible.

26 WEDNESDAY *Moon Age Day 23 Moon Sign Aries*

This could well be a very good time to plan a day away, or even to take one at a moment's notice. You won't be happy to be kept in the same place all the time and can easily become bored with routines. There are potential gains to be made through casual contacts and unusual business deals.

27 THURSDAY *Moon Age Day 24 Moon Sign Aries*

Around now there could be encounters with potential new friends and you should not turn down the chance to get together with like-minded people. The very gregarious side of your nature is now clearly on display and you have what it takes to impress those who can do you some good in a financial sense.

28 FRIDAY *Moon Age Day 25 Moon Sign Taurus*

Try to seek out new social contacts at this time. This year is very important in terms of making new friends and so watch out in particular for people who are on the same wavelength as you. There could be a stop–start feeling to today that can only be countered by applying yourself fully to the task at hand.

29 SATURDAY *Moon Age Day 26 Moon Sign Taurus*

Benefits may come through relationships and right now you should be feeling a safe and secure bond with loved ones. There will be time for romance in your life, even though you may feel that this is at the expense of practical matters. Tomorrow is another day so for the moment simply enjoy being cosseted.

30 SUNDAY

Moon Age Day 27   Moon Sign Gemini

Where important work is to be carried out there are likely to be a few tensions, even though these are not coming from your direction. This is a time when you can win over others fairly easily and yet you can also be very effective when doing things on your own. The flexibility of the Archer is now definitely on display.

July
2019

1 MONDAY
Moon Age Day 28   Moon Sign Gemini

Things tail off a little for a couple of days but since most of the difficulties are with regard to career and practical matters, if you are able to spend a couple of days relaxing, you may hardly notice the lunar low this time around. Sit down and work out a few details to put into practice further down the line.

2 TUESDAY
Moon Age Day 0   Moon Sign Gemini

You tend to think that you will be beaten, even before you start and that's not at all a good sign for the Archer. Don't worry. These trends are only for today and as long as you don't have any major decisions to make, all will be well. If you are expected to pass an opinion – simply fudge for a day or two.

3 WEDNESDAY
Moon Age Day 1   Moon Sign Cancer

All of a sudden your dominant personality comes to the fore and is something you will need to control at all costs. It's not the side of you that some people want to see. A little co-operation can go a long way and is certainly useful where work is concerned. Your creative potential remains good and you turn heads in this area of life.

4 THURSDAY
Moon Age Day 2   Moon Sign Cancer

During this period you have plenty of practical energy and can easily sort situations out whilst others are still thinking about them. It's a fact of life this year that you are sometimes going to encounter the jealousy of others. There isn't much you can do about this situation except to accept that it happens.

5 FRIDAY
Moon Age Day 3   Moon Sign Leo

Stand by for a really pleasurable day but one that demands so much of you in every sense that you may end it exhausted. Dashing about from pillar to post, you might not be spending as much time with the one you love the best as you would wish. Explain yourself and little or no damage is likely to be done.

6 SATURDAY
Moon Age Day 4   Moon Sign Leo

This could prove to be an especially good time with regard to goals and objectives. Financial security is also likely to be on your mind and you will be doing all you can to make sure there will soon be more money coming in. It ought to be possible to do some sort of deal that offsets previous monetary hiccups.

7 SUNDAY
Moon Age Day 5   Moon Sign Virgo

Monetary gains are the name of the game today and you will be doing everything you can to improve the family finances. If someone is spending too liberally you are going to have to tell them, even if to do so is somewhat embarrassing. Ease back on this mood later and end the day with a proper treat.

8 MONDAY   ☿
Moon Age Day 6   Moon Sign Virgo

Professional matters, though containing a few challenges, seem to work out especially well for you today. Not that you are concentrating solely on this area of your life. On the contrary you know how to have fun and would willingly join in with any social gathering that is taking place.

9 TUESDAY   ☿
Moon Age Day 7   Moon Sign Libra

You may be actively concerned about the welfare of loved ones right now, though this could possibly be without any real justification. You need to look at situations quite carefully before you start worrying about them. If you have a slightly frazzled start to the day, stop, get your breath and start again slowly.

10 WEDNESDAY ☿   *Moon Age Day 8   Moon Sign Libra*

There is now likely to be a new focus on finance with a 'me and mine' attitude on your part that you don't normally display. You won't have to try too hard to increase your financial standing but it could mean being a bit more mercenary than has been the case of late. Friends may prove to be quite mystifying at the moment.

11 THURSDAY ☿   *Moon Age Day 9   Moon Sign Scorpio*

News tends to be encouraging and short trips can be especially rewarding. People you don't get to see very often could be paying visits and all in all there isn't going to be a great deal of time to concentrate on professional or practical matters. Treat today as some sort of holiday and let others take the strain.

12 FRIDAY ☿   *Moon Age Day 10   Moon Sign Scorpio*

You may feel like dwelling on the past today, which isn't really going to be of much help in a general sense. Better by far to commit yourself to the present and the future and to concentrate on what matters the most to your life as it stands. Nostalgia is fine in its place but is no alternative to simply getting stuck in.

13 SATURDAY ☿ *Moon Age Day 11   Moon Sign Sagittarius*

With the Moon now in your zodiac sign this is the time of the month to pile on the action. Be brave, bold and dynamic and determined to succeed in almost anything. You will find others helpful and quite willing to offer you their advice and practical assistance but in the main you are very self-possessed.

14 SUNDAY ☿ *Moon Age Day 12   Moon Sign Sagittarius*

This is a really good time for increased influence over life generally, though this being a Sunday it's possible that social matters will predominate over professional ones. What an ideal time this would be to take a journey, even if it's one that is planned at the last minute. Stay in the company of exciting people.

15 MONDAY ☿ *Moon Age Day 13* *Moon Sign Capricorn*

Under today's trends you will approach life with great gusto and a determination that is second to none. Whilst others are worrying about their limitations, you are committing yourself fully to getting ahead. All matters to do with communication are much enhanced by the present planetary line up.

16 TUESDAY ☿ *Moon Age Day 14* *Moon Sign Capricorn*

It is just possible that situations beyond your own control undermine your ability to control your own destiny today. Avoid being overbearing at home, especially with people who might be a bit grumpy but who do have your best interests at heart. Someone who is fun to be around could visit later in the day.

17 WEDNESDAY ☿ *Moon Age Day 15* *Moon Sign Capricorn*

Avoid disputes at home and if necessary stay away from potential trouble. If you do insist on arguing with anyone, make sure you understand what you are talking about first. Not everyone is going to be equally helpful today so try to seek out those who are positive and avoid those who are negative.

18 THURSDAY ☿ *Moon Age Day 16* *Moon Sign Aquarius*

Review past efforts for the best chance of getting ahead right now. Contributing to your own eventual success is possible but you won't get everything you want without relying on others more than you usually do. Your confidence could be high in some matters but distinctly lacking in others.

19 FRIDAY ☿ *Moon Age Day 17* *Moon Sign Aquarius*

Someone who is special to you has a message or two to impart at the moment. This might be a slightly frustrating day in one way or another, not least of all because the people you rely on in a professional sense are either missing or else not performing to the best of their ability. Attitude is very important in practical matters.

20 SATURDAY ☿ *Moon Age Day 18* *Moon Sign Pisces*

People you get along with well are likely to be coming into your life and they might bring with the chance to get something you have wanted for a while. Attitude is very important today because if you show people that you know what you are doing and that you are trustworthy, you can get almost anything.

21 SUNDAY ☿ *Moon Age Day 19* *Moon Sign Pisces*

It is possible for you to put your practical thoughts into words that the world understands. Not only this but it appears that some of your colleagues and even superiors might be actively seeking you out. Stay away from situations over which you can have no influence and which might prove awkward.

22 MONDAY ☿ *Moon Age Day 20* *Moon Sign Pisces*

Present trends offer solutions to problems that have been a bind for some time. You think clearly and have an ability to get to the heart of any matter almost instantly. Others will be envious of this talent but they won't be beyond picking your brains when it best suits their purposes.

23 TUESDAY ☿ *Moon Age Day 21* *Moon Sign Aries*

Those higher up the professional tree than you are might prove to be especially useful at the moment but only because of your own attitude, which is positive and helpful. Significant people are apt to enter your life around now and bring with them some interesting potential changes of direction for you.

24 WEDNESDAY ☿ *Moon Age Day 22* *Moon Sign Aries*

Challenges and career moves are easy to deal with and this is a time during which you don't mind at all taking on new responsibilities. You can be very impressive when in company so don't be surprised if others are paying you some significant compliments. Present trends are also good when it comes to love and romance.

25 THURSDAY ☿ *Moon Age Day 23   Moon Sign Taurus*

Matters connected with friendships are positively highlighted and it ought to be a piece of cake to get others to do your bidding today. Not that you are being selfish because most of your present intentions suit others as much as yourself. For most this will be a socially rewarding day, with plenty of romantic possibilities too.

26 FRIDAY ☿ *Moon Age Day 24   Moon Sign Taurus*

Professional circles bring new friendships and new ways of looking at old situations. What is most noticeable at the moment is the way you cut through red tape and get to the heart of any matter. People will be pleased to follow your lead at the moment so the time has come to put a few plans into action.

27 SATURDAY ☿ *Moon Age Day 25   Moon Sign Taurus*

It could feel that your emotional security is being threatened in some way but even so you must avoid hanging on to the past. Project your mind forward and in doing so you will make slow and steady progress. Anything old may interest at the moment and you might enjoy visiting galleries or museums.

28 SUNDAY ☿ *Moon Age Day 26   Moon Sign Gemini*

Progress is apt to be rather slow whilst the lunar low is around, so much so that today and tomorrow mark a time during which you ought to be thinking rather than doing. Don't be too quick to take on anything new and you certainly should not be pushing the bounds of the possible until the middle of next week.

29 MONDAY ☿ *Moon Age Day 27   Moon Sign Gemini*

Keep to tried and tested methods of doing things because the new and radical is not the way forward at the moment. The greatest happiness today comes from being close to those you love, many of whom will be actively putting themselves out in order to make you happy. Routines might seem comfortable.

30 TUESDAY ☿ *Moon Age Day 28   Moon Sign Cancer*

Good fortune seems to attend many of your efforts at the moment and now you are better placed to get ahead. Others are looking to you for support and inspiration and you have increased energy that can be used in a number of different ways. A new month lies in store and you will want to be ready for all it offers.

31 WEDNESDAY ☿ *Moon Age Day 0   Moon Sign Cancer*

It could prove profitable now to speak your mind. You will do so diplomatically and this means you will be listened to, especially by superiors. Stand by a decision you have made even if this means working harder than usual, but also recognise when it would be better to be flexible.

2019

1 THURSDAY
Moon Age Day 1   Moon Sign Leo

You will gain from a variety of interests today and can be sure that events are generally on your side. The attitude of those you encounter ought to be good and you have what it takes to make the best sort of impression. Family disagreements may be breaking out but you are unlikely to be a part of any of them.

2 FRIDAY
Moon Age Day 2   Moon Sign Leo

Prioritise today and don't allow yourself to get sidetracked by irrelevant details. Make the most of new opportunities at work and do your best to create a good impression. Someone may be watching at the moment, even if you don't realise it, and how you come across will stand you in good stead later.

3 SATURDAY
Moon Age Day 3   Moon Sign Virgo

Make the best of information that comes your way, especially from colleagues or friends. Others won't always see the potential opportunities but you certainly will. Riding the ups and downs of life is quite easy at the moment and you won't be swayed once your mind is made up.

4 SUNDAY
Moon Age Day 4   Moon Sign Virgo

You may have to accommodate the needs of others today and that will probably mean you don't have too much time for yourself. That won't worry you too much as long as you feel you are getting a good deal out of life. Don't allow a lack of confidence to put you off tackling a job at home.

5 MONDAY   *Moon Age Day 5   Moon Sign Libra*

Events may open up some new ideas and with some very good trends on the way this is definitely the time to get going. You may need to adopt new attitudes and policies and if so should be happy to do whatever it takes to get on in life generally. Friends will make demands but they are easily settled in the main.

6 TUESDAY   *Moon Age Day 6   Moon Sign Libra*

Travel and communication are both extremely well highlighted at the moment and you can't wait to get out there and have a good time. You may have chosen this time for a holiday and if so you were wise indeed. Company tends to be entertaining and made up of people who have the ability to make you laugh.

7 WEDNESDAY   *Moon Age Day 7   Moon Sign Scorpio*

Communicating your ideas to others is not difficult now and that applies whether you are dealing with bosses, colleagues or friends. On the romantic front you find just the right words to express your feelings and could turn out to be quite poetic at this time. Don't let younger family members aggravate you; you might be playing into their hands.

8 THURSDAY   *Moon Age Day 8   Moon Sign Scorpio*

You won't get too much out of casual contacts at the moment and tend to go more for deep and meaningful attachments. Colleagues might be slightly difficult to deal with and that green-eyed monster jealousy could be part of the reason. You make a big impression and not everyone likes or respects the fact.

9 FRIDAY   *Moon Age Day 9   Moon Sign Sagittarius*

This is the time of the month for thinking big and not at all the sort of period during which you should hide your light in any way. There are gains coming from expected and unexpected directions and this is definitely a period during which you need to keep your eyes open. You tend to act quickly now.

10 SATURDAY   *Moon Age Day 10   Moon Sign Sagittarius*

Make this a day to win friends and to influence people generally. You won't be slow to make progress when it is offered and you might see opportunities that others do not. Confidence is definitely on the increase and you have what it takes to get ahead. If you are at work, you could well be suggesting better ways of doing things.

11 SUNDAY   *Moon Age Day 11   Moon Sign Sagittarius*

Family members will now be doing all they can to make you happy and comfortable, though you may decide that this is the last thing you want as you plunge into just about any excitement you can think of. You won't take kindly now to being told what to do and set out instead to please yourself.

12 MONDAY   *Moon Age Day 12   Moon Sign Capricorn*

Making practical progress is now partly down to the way others are willing to work on your behalf. The choice is yours because not everyone concerned is a person you care for very much. Either you can be one hundred percent honest and struggle a little more, or else tell the odd white lie and find you are getting on really well.

13 TUESDAY   *Moon Age Day 13   Moon Sign Capricorn*

It looks as though you are enjoying more personal freedom now and that means making the most of life. It is quality that matters today, rather than quantity and so whatever you do, you will want to do it to the best of your ability. Congratulations might be in order somewhere in the family or amongst friends.

14 WEDNESDAY   *Moon Age Day 14   Moon Sign Aquarius*

Someone you meet today, probably in a professional capacity, can have a tremendous bearing on the way your mind is working. Today is not a time to stand on ceremony but a period during which you have to let people know the way you see things. You can be relied upon to use some diplomacy all the same.

15 THURSDAY   *Moon Age Day 15   Moon Sign Aquarius*

There could be a good chance to have a special time with a colleague today and an ability to happily mix business with pleasure. Group situations work well in a professional and a social sense because all the sharing qualities of your Sagittarian nature are now clearly demonstrating themselves.

16 FRIDAY   *Moon Age Day 16   Moon Sign Aquarius*

Your imagination might not be quite as well connected to reality today as is usually the case. If you are offered something that looks like a bargain that is too good to be true, turn all your powers of discrimination on the situation. Trends suggest that you should be sceptical as possible around this time.

17 SATURDAY   *Moon Age Day 17   Moon Sign Pisces*

It is probable that your social life will be very busy this weekend and that means not having too much time to get on with the practicalities of life. That doesn't really matter as weekends are made for relaxation, so do whatever takes your fancy. There are some very interesting people around now.

18 SUNDAY   *Moon Age Day 18   Moon Sign Pisces*

A breezy attitude predominates and it isn't at all hard for you to take life fully in your stride. Get out of the house and find some way to blow any cobwebs away. You won't get everything you want today in a practical sense and so it might be best to shelve such considerations, at least until the start of a new week tomorrow.

19 MONDAY   *Moon Age Day 19   Moon Sign Aries*

There could be a minor setback if you don't watch out today and as a result this is a time during which it would not be sensible to take too many chances in life. Listen to the advice of those you trust and settle for a low-key sort of day, though one that still offers a good deal of potential personal satisfaction.

20 TUESDAY   *Moon Age Day 20   Moon Sign Aries*

Certain tensions could arise at home, probably because of the way a loved one is behaving. Once you have offered your point of view there probably isn't much else to be done and you will just have to wait and see. Some of the best possible moments today come via friends rather than relatives.

21 WEDNESDAY   *Moon Age Day 21   Moon Sign Aries*

There may be times today when you can make a real difference to the way those around you are thinking, and this is particularly true with regard to work colleagues and past associates. Set out to have a good time. You might have been rather too serious for your own good of late and need to redress the balance.

22 THURSDAY   *Moon Age Day 22   Moon Sign Taurus*

Social matters should bring some promising new developments. You are friendly with just about anyone and more than willing to share what you have. Although there may be very slight hiccups in your romantic attachments, when it matters the most your partner or sweetheart is likely to come up trumps.

23 FRIDAY   *Moon Age Day 23   Moon Sign Taurus*

Your imagination is easily stimulated around now and you won't have any difficulty at all following the possibilities that come about as a result of a daydream. When it comes to proving your case in an issue that has been on your mind for a while however, what you need is evidence and that might not be too easy to discover.

24 SATURDAY   *Moon Age Day 24   Moon Sign Gemini*

The Moon is now in your opposite zodiac sign and as a result you find yourself somewhat subdued. Things won't improve all that much tomorrow either but it really depends on your attitude and your understanding of present astrological trends. If you don't expect too much, you won't be disappointed.

25 SUNDAY   *Moon Age Day 25   Moon Sign Gemini*

Although this Sunday does offer some benefits, it isn't going to be the best day you will ever experience. Keep responsibilities to a minimum and allow others to do some of the work. The less you take on your own shoulders, the more likely you are to enjoy the ride. Plan for an active and enterprising week ahead.

26 MONDAY   *Moon Age Day 26   Moon Sign Cancer*

Some objectives might simply fail to materialise, which is why you need to keep your options well and truly open at this time. The attitude of friends or even relatives might be difficult to understand today and you will have to ask them to explain themselves if you are going to get on-side with them.

27 TUESDAY   *Moon Age Day 27   Moon Sign Cancer*

The planetary focus at the moment seems to be quite definitely on the past and emotional influences are likely to crop up all the time. Anything that removes you from the limelight turns out to be a good thing because you are in a very contemplative frame of mind and in the main might want to be left alone.

28 WEDNESDAY   *Moon Age Day 28   Moon Sign Leo*

Try to avoid too much daydreaming at the moment because what you really need today is concrete action. A few rules might get on your nerves and, if so, you will be spending a great deal of time working out how to circumnavigate them altogether. There could be a mischievous side to the Archer at present.

29 THURSDAY   *Moon Age Day 29   Moon Sign Leo*

Your social life could be the place to look for success today because you probably won't find it all that readily in a professional or practical sense. Friends should be warm and encouraging but there isn't really too much point in pushing yourself towards any chosen destination until tomorrow.

30 FRIDAY
Moon Age Day 0   Moon Sign Virgo

Some reorganisation may be required and if so you are just in the right frame of mind to take it on. The results ought to be more than worth the effort and you are steadily getting towards a new way of looking at old aspects of life. Allow a younger relative a little more leeway than you have been doing.

31 SATURDAY
Moon Age Day 1   Moon Sign Virgo

With plenty to celebrate at home you have what it takes to make this a really good day all round. Confidence isn't lacking when you need it the most and you are likely to be showing your friendliest face to the world at large. This is the Archer at its best and it is something that others find distinctly captivating.

September
2019

1 SUNDAY
Moon Age Day 2   Moon Sign Libra

Planetary trends show that social and co-operative ventures ought to be working out very well for you at the moment. Although there may be an issue to resolve early in the day it shouldn't be very long before you are working to your best ability and solving a few other problems on the way.

2 MONDAY
Moon Age Day 3   Moon Sign Libra

A lift to your spirits comes along today and there should be some strong social highlights to be enjoyed. An arrangement that is likely to be made by friends might lead to some really interesting interludes, though it is possible that some of these won't actually arrive until later in the week.

3 TUESDAY
Moon Age Day 4   Moon Sign Scorpio

Don't become over idealistic about a romantic issue. It is possible that you are not seeing things quite as clearly now as would usually be the case and some impartial advice from a friend could be in order. Make sure your expectations of life are fairly realistic around this time.

4 WEDNESDAY
Moon Age Day 5   Moon Sign Scorpio

Relationships could prove to be a little troublesome today. In your mind the fault is not yours but you are reasonable by nature and so will come to accept that it takes two to tango. Don't be too quick to make a judgement about a friend who is behaving rather strangely. You may not know all the circumstances.

5 THURSDAY   *Moon Age Day 6   Moon Sign Scorpio*

Today should be a day of greater introspection and evaluation and you will be quite happy to accept that you cannot always be noisy and active. You want to look at things closely and won't be so keen to push ahead with plans until you are certain in your own mind that they are going to work out well.

6 FRIDAY   *Moon Age Day 7   Moon Sign Sagittarius*

Today is favourable for all sorts of new plans and for consolidating past gains in original ways. You are likely to be as sociable as ever and you show great flair when it comes to organising almost anything. Any negative traits of the last few days are nothing but a dull memory as you push forward on all fronts.

7 SATURDAY   *Moon Age Day 8   Moon Sign Sagittarius*

Someone may put the dampener on relationships for you, or at least they are going to try. If you are aware of what is going on, you can also do something positive to prevent it. If matters appertaining to your love life are somehow up in the air, this would be a good time to sort matters out once and for all.

8 SUNDAY   *Moon Age Day 9   Moon Sign Capricorn*

It looks as though you are going to be especially assertive, even somewhat pushy at the moment, a fact that could certainly come as a surprise to your nearest and dearest. The Archer has been as pleasant as the day is long so when you get assertive, those who know you best are naturally unsettled.

9 MONDAY   *Moon Age Day 10   Moon Sign Capricorn*

Social matters are helpfully highlighted in today's chart making this a good day to mix with others in all areas of your life. There should be less internal confusion now and this diminishes even more over the next few days. Try to co-operate at work because to do so can be a definite boon.

10 TUESDAY   *Moon Age Day 11   Moon Sign Aquarius*

Loved ones could prove rather difficult to understand today and a little extra effort on your part may be necessary. You might have to put the brake on some social activities for the moment or at least reorganise things in some way. At work you could make progress without even realising that you are doing so.

11 WEDNESDAY   *Moon Age Day 12   Moon Sign Aquarius*

You now have a great deal of energy that is available to put into whatever takes your fancy. Although there may not be anything particularly important happening at present, you are in a good position to enjoy yourself and also to bring a good deal of happiness into the lives of the people with whom you make contact.

12 THURSDAY   *Moon Age Day 13   Moon Sign Aquarius*

Your mind is sharp, making this an especially good day for study or detailed work of any kind. You will be able to come to terms with issues that confused you in the past and won't be at all lazy. Social trends continue to look good and some of the best possibilities arise from a prospective journey.

13 FRIDAY   *Moon Age Day 14   Moon Sign Pisces*

For most of today you will be feeling very positive about yourself and can make the best of impressions on the world at large. This is a period during which you want to enjoy yourself and there won't be too much time for deep thinking. The future seems to be an unwritten book and for the moment you are happy to have it so.

14 SATURDAY   *Moon Age Day 15   Moon Sign Pisces*

You may now see the fruits of recent efforts in a more positive light, though you can still expect quite a few twists and turns in the way your mind is working. Material plans now tend to take shape very well but a certain amount of modification is necessary if you really want to score successes socially.

15 SUNDAY   *Moon Age Day 16   Moon Sign Aries*

You might be forced to fall back on your own resources a little today but that's no bad thing and you tend to cope with the situation very well indeed. You won't be too keen to listen to the advice of people you haven't exactly liked in the past but if what they are saying is the truth you really should at least take note.

16 MONDAY   *Moon Age Day 17   Moon Sign Aries*

The big wide world can now seem very inspiring and you won't take much encouragement to be a part of it. The weather should still be fairly good and you will have a great desire to get out and about. Concentrating on work won't be easy but you will be quite happy to simply find yourself some fun.

17 TUESDAY   *Moon Age Day 18   Moon Sign Aries*

This is a period during which you will probably have some time to spend on yourself. The Archer is now a little quieter than of late, giving you time to think and to plan. Although there are plenty of potential invitations coming in, generally speaking you will be happier to watch and wait for a while.

18 WEDNESDAY   *Moon Age Day 19   Moon Sign Taurus*

The domestic scene is likely to be far busier today and you are in for a very active sort of Sunday. Confirming some of your earlier suspicions, you are well ahead of the game generally and able to use your intuition to assess people and situations. Look out for matters of love, which could take you very much by surprise today.

19 THURSDAY   *Moon Age Day 20   Moon Sign Taurus*

This is probably the very best day this week for being at home and for doing simple things that satisfy you. You benefit from a deep sense of belonging and will be enjoying the company of family members more than that of friends. Enjoy what should be a relaxing interlude, if you can.

20 FRIDAY
Moon Age Day 21   Moon Sign Gemini

With the lunar low around today you could become somewhat disillusioned, though if you realise what is going on in an astrological sense you will also be quite aware that this is a very temporary matter. Stick to routines. These will suit you for the next couple of days and they offer a sense of security.

21 SATURDAY
Moon Age Day 22   Moon Sign Gemini

Avoid making too many decisions again today and simply go with the flow. There are people around who can even make the period of the lunar low a joy but you have to give them the benefit of the doubt. Ask for something you want today because someone close to you is in a generous mood.

22 SUNDAY
Moon Age Day 23   Moon Sign Gemini

Look out for a heavily competitive element this Sunday. How this has a bearing on your life will depend on your own circumstances. For example, if you work at the weekend you could find that you are pushing towards advancement. On the other hand socially inclined Sagittarians may be taking part in sport.

23 MONDAY
Moon Age Day 24   Moon Sign Cancer

Much energy can now be put into getting what you want from life. You have boundless energy and a determination to get on well, even when the odds seem to be stacked against you. There is hardly any obstacle around now that cannot be removed by sheer force of will, together with your singular charm.

24 TUESDAY
Moon Age Day 25   Moon Sign Cancer

There is just a possibility that you will be slightly impetuous when it comes to spending money and that could presently be a mistake. Before you make any major purchase stop and think. Is it something you really need or are you simply compromising because what you really want isn't available?

25 WEDNESDAY
Moon Age Day 26   Moon Sign Leo

You should enjoy a higher degree of emotional contentment now and perhaps this has more to do with the way others seem to be behaving than it does to do with your own personality. Once again you are likely to settle for a reasonably quite time, secure in the bosom of your family and not needing too much else.

26 THURSDAY
Moon Age Day 27   Moon Sign Leo

Around this time your home life continues to be enjoyable and you are making the most of family relationships. In some respects you might be all fingers and thumbs but that's something that happens to Sagittarians occasionally. More haste and less speed should probably be your motto for the moment.

27 FRIDAY
Moon Age Day 28   Moon Sign Virgo

You should be enjoying domestic happiness, whilst at the same time itching to do something different. Whilst you don't want to upset the apple cart at home, you need all sorts of stimulation in order to get the best out of your life. Confidence boosting exercises at work should have the desired effect.

28 SATURDAY
Moon Age Day 0   Moon Sign Virgo

Trends this weekend are geared almost exclusively towards leisure and pleasure and you really do need to find time to do something that pleases you. What won't impress you at all is being constantly at the beck and call of people who are quite capable of doing things for themselves. You might have to be a little blunt.

29 SUNDAY
Moon Age Day 1   Moon Sign Libra

It could appear that there is something missing today and you will have to work hard if you want to get ahead. There are no really bad astrological trends around today, but there are not many good ones either. In the end you need to make your own luck for a day or two and also spend quite a lot of time with joyful people.

30 MONDAY   *Moon Age Day 2   Moon Sign Libra*

You may be showing off a little today – not that this is particularly peculiar for the Archer. All the same, you could easily give the wrong impression so do let someone else stand in the limelight, at least for a while. There's no doubt about your popularity but don't milk it.

October 2019

1 TUESDAY
Moon Age Day 3   Moon Sign Scorpio

In a continuation of trends from the end of last week, you will find things that are happening out in the big, wide world more alluring than domestic matters, even though those are running smoothly. However, you won't be too keen to start any major new project until after tomorrow.

2 WEDNESDAY
Moon Age Day 4   Moon Sign Scorpio

Peak professional influences are present and everything looks right to launch a new incentive at work. No matter how lowly you consider your position to be, you can make it better now. In a social sense it isn't quite so easy to conform to expectations and you definitely want to present a fresh image.

3 THURSDAY
Moon Age Day 5   Moon Sign Sagittarius

The lunar high redresses anything that was of balance and fits you for better things today. As Thursday dawns you are keen to get on and will be pushing the bounds of the possible on every possible occasion. You won't find everyone on your side but the ones who are not are probably not relevant.

4 FRIDAY
Moon Age Day 6   Moon Sign Sagittarius

If you feel like you are spending too much, you could use your energy and ingenuity to find ways to get what you want without parting with too much cash. What matters now is how much fun you can get from life and you are certainly in the right frame of mind to bring others round to your own particular point of view.

5 SATURDAY · Moon Age Day 7 · Moon Sign Capricorn

Even though you might not presently consider that you are working at your best, you might discover otherwise if others want to take a leaf from your book. There are possible financial gains around this time, one or two of which may come from directions you certainly would not have expected.

6 SUNDAY · Moon Age Day 8 · Moon Sign Capricorn

You may need to rid yourself of a situation that seems to be holding you back. It might be necessary to sit and think about such matters before you take action because present astrological trends may incline you to act with haste. Nevertheless, when you have made up your mind, go for it.

7 MONDAY · Moon Age Day 9 · Moon Sign Capricorn

Romance may well be in full bloom right now and you may feel the need to spend an autumn day out and about with your partner or someone who is now becoming more important to you. The Sagittarian mind is in full flow and anything to do with either speaking or writing is especially favoured at this time.

8 TUESDAY · Moon Age Day 10 · Moon Sign Aquarius

Romance is strong on your personal agenda and the opportunities that exist to express your affections are great. You certainly don't lack ego, but you express it in a very positive way and one that proves attractive to many other people. The immediate is not half as rewarding as forward planning for most Archers now.

9 WEDNESDAY · Moon Age Day 11 · Moon Sign Aquarius

You could have some good ideas at work today, and as a result may be able to improve systems and operations. No matter what you do for a living, you now have the opportunity to streamline situations and to get on better as a result. The Archer is in the mood to compartmentalise different aspects of life but be aware that others might find your reasoning a little unusual.

10 THURSDAY   *Moon Age Day 12   Moon Sign Pisces*

Trends indicate harmony in and around your home and so this might seem to be the best place to be. Although you are probably right, there are matters in the outside world that still demand your attention, so you can expect real peace and quiet to be hard to come by. Take matters in your stride.

11 FRIDAY   *Moon Age Day 13   Moon Sign Pisces*

Your love life keeps you busy at the same time as a great sense of freedom breaks over you. If you are facing challenges, these won't bother you at all. This is not a good time to put off any task that you should be getting on with right now. Trends indicate that the end of a significant chapter in your life is close.

12 SATURDAY   *Moon Age Day 14   Moon Sign Pisces*

Material duties may limit your options today and you certainly won't feel yourself to have the freedom of yesterday, or that you would wish. This is not going to be the most startling weekend of the year generally but there are gains if you look for them. It's important to do things you already know you are good at.

13 SUNDAY   *Moon Age Day 15   Moon Sign Aries*

The only thing that is likely to get you down today is an emotional issue you can't remedy. Stay away from that and compared with yesterday the world should be your oyster. Your decision-making abilities are now sharp and focused and you have a better idea regarding the future.

14 MONDAY   *Moon Age Day 16   Moon Sign Aries*

Though you seem to be well on top of most practical issues, today has a lot to do with enjoyment. If you haven't exactly been painting the town red of late, today you can put that right. Someone who has been very special to you for a long time is now likely to let you know what their feelings are.

15 TUESDAY   *Moon Age Day 17   Moon Sign Taurus*

Things at work could turn out to be the opposite of what you expected. Don't be too quick to judge people or situations and do what you can to remain in the public eye. Although you can be criticised for talking about things you don't understand, this is not likely to happen too often so get on with it.

16 WEDNESDAY   *Moon Age Day 18   Moon Sign Taurus*

A major new focus is now on leisure and romantic matters. With everything working generally well you should be able to see quite easily how attractive you are to others. There are distinct gains to be made at this time from simply being what you naturally are. Personalities abound, both at work and socially.

17 THURSDAY   *Moon Age Day 19   Moon Sign Taurus*

Financial objectives may gain some planetary assistance today so this would be a good time to look at money and to work out how best to plan for the future. At the same time there is a strong social quality to the day and you won't have any trouble in mixing business with pleasure.

18 FRIDAY   *Moon Age Day 20   Moon Sign Gemini*

With the lunar low now in evidence you should avoid getting gloomy about situations that are clearly temporary. Give yourself fully to the task in hand but don't expect to push down many barriers around now. Social trends are good and especially when you are mixing with people you already know and like.

19 SATURDAY   *Moon Age Day 21   Moon Sign Gemini*

Since your judgement tends to be marred by present trends, it would be better not to take decisions that you can't revoke later. Neither is this a good time for signing documents unless you have looked at them very carefully indeed. You might have to plan a push at work but don't start shoving until Monday.

20 SUNDAY   *Moon Age Day 22   Moon Sign Cancer*

Settling for second best is not usually your way but that seems to be what you are doing at the moment. Routines may look quite attractive and you will plod along through the day in a reasonably happy frame of mind just as long as you don't try to push yourself too much. Try to maintain a good sense of humour.

21 MONDAY   *Moon Age Day 23   Moon Sign Cancer*

A period of greater efficiency and higher energy is now on the way. With everything to play for this ought to be a crackerjack of a week at work and you will be doing everything you can to make those around you as happy as you are. You realise instinctively at the moment that attitude is everything.

22 TUESDAY   *Moon Age Day 24   Moon Sign Leo*

There ought to be plenty of ways you can feed your ego at the moment, though you are also showing a degree of modesty. Nevertheless you need to be preened now and again and to know how important you are to those around you. Fishing for compliments might bring a bigger than expected catch today.

23 WEDNESDAY   *Moon Age Day 25   Moon Sign Leo*

If you have wanted to make any sort of fresh starts or improvements and changes to your home, this is probably the best time to get cracking. Enlist the support of family members and plan what you are going to do but at the end of the day it's really a case of taking the bull by the horns.

24 THURSDAY   *Moon Age Day 26   Moon Sign Virgo*

This is probably the best day of the month in which to express your love for someone very special indeed. Although you might be committed to work, you are also entering a period in which a sense of personal freedom is especially important. As a result you should to try and arrange some sort of break later in the day.

25 FRIDAY
Moon Age Day 27   Moon Sign Virgo

The Archer is inclined to be a little self-indulgent today and certainly quite inward looking. Your present idea of being selfish is simply spending a little time on your own and there is nothing wrong with that. In any case, some of the ideas that come into your mind today can be put into action under the more progressive trends of tomorrow.

26 SATURDAY
Moon Age Day 28   Moon Sign Libra

With a more competitive streak now firmly on the display you will want to push forward on all fronts. This might not be especially easy and you will need to use that extra bit of effort that is necessary to get ahead of some of the small difficulties that surround you. Acting on impulse comes as second nature.

27 SUNDAY
Moon Age Day 0   Moon Sign Libra

You are willing to work hard and to do whatever it takes to get to your chosen destination. Don't get bogged down with details today but stick to the main plan because it's the big picture that counts. By the evening you will probably be quite happy to relax in the bosom of your family.

28 MONDAY
Moon Age Day 1   Moon Sign Scorpio

For much of the month you have made fairly good progress in material matters and now comes a time when it seems important to consolidate all your efforts up to now. Some ingenuity is obvious and you may be decisive about your actions. That might not seem like much but it's very important to you.

29 TUESDAY
Moon Age Day 2   Moon Sign Scorpio

A boost to your ego could come as a result of the compliments that fall into your lap. The more you mix with others, the greater are the potential rewards that could come your way. Although your attention is somewhat divided at the moment you can still concentrate if you try.

30 WEDNESDAY   *Moon Age Day 3   Moon Sign Sagittarius*

Positive thinking really does pay off well today. The lunar high brings so much light and energy into your life, virtually nothing is beyond your capabilities. Something that has been at the back of your mind and which has been troubling you of late can now be addressed and settled.

31 THURSDAY   *Moon Age Day 4   Moon Sign Sagittarius*

An element of serendipity shows itself in your life at the moment. Even when you are not particularly looking for them, opportunities should come along. Just about everyone seems willing to help you towards your objectives and there is no doubt at all that a little cheek goes a very long way.

November

2019

1 FRIDAY ☿ *Moon Age Day 5 Moon Sign Sagittarius*

This is the time of the month during which progress is most likely. Don't settle for too little but go out to get what you really want from life. You are progressive, positive and very cheerful. All practical issues can be addressed now in the almost certain knowledge that you are able to succeed.

2 SATURDAY ☿ *Moon Age Day 6 Moon Sign Capricorn*

Attracting the good things in life ought to be fairly easy, even if those around you are still rather hesitant. The one thing that can definitely be said about your zodiac sign is that it doesn't like to wait for anything, which is why you are concentrating your efforts and forging ahead no matter what the circumstances.

3 SUNDAY ☿ *Moon Age Day 7 Moon Sign Capricorn*

You are a natural master of ceremonies, which is why you take command at social functions and the like. The Archer is a child of the moment so don't expect to be overly pleased if family members want you to make up your mind about Christmas already. You are very friendly at present but still anxious to get things done.

4 MONDAY ☿ *Moon Age Day 8 Moon Sign Aquarius*

The atmosphere at work looks as though it will be harmonious and you are not likely to encounter too many problems today. Make sure that you are confident in yourself before you embark on a new project about which you know nothing. If necessary, ask someone who knows better than you do.

5 TUESDAY ☿ *Moon Age Day 9   Moon Sign Aquarius*

Work matters and the general progress you are making are well accentuated but there may be slight stumbling blocks to be dealt with on the way. Despite this you can still make significant progress and won't be held back, even when those closest to you seem to be running on half speed.

6 WEDNESDAY ☿ *Moon Age Day 10   Moon Sign Pisces*

New relationships are likely to begin around this time. These won't necessarily be romantic in nature but they should prove to be quite fortunate. Acting on impulse might be problematic but you will sort out slight difficulties as and when you come across them. Avoid games of chance today.

7 THURSDAY ☿ *Moon Age Day 11   Moon Sign Pisces*

Friendly co-operation with others is what counts now. It might be difficult to get ahead in a practical sense, but you should be able to arrange new strategies and will have time to think things through. This is the sort of day you will want to split, so that it's possible to have fun, whilst at the same time enjoying some genuine relaxation.

8 FRIDAY ☿ *Moon Age Day 12   Moon Sign Pisces*

You should now be feeling secure about yourself. As a result you will argue your corner very well and with much justification. What you won't be able to stand at the moment is being told what to do by people who have no real idea about you, your life or, more importantly, your capabilities.

9 SATURDAY ☿ *Moon Age Day 13   Moon Sign Aries*

This would be a good day to be working on a long, time-consuming project. You have plenty of patience and enough resilience to see things through to the end. The sheer amount of effort you are prepared to put in to something you really want is almost monumental and far surpasses the Archer's usual staying power.

10 SUNDAY ☿ *Moon Age Day 14 Moon Sign Aries*

There are some indications of success on the way, even if you have to peek out from under the bedclothes of life to see them. You won't be shy when it comes to examining every nook and cranny of any circumstance to find what you want and you are as nosey as the Archer is ever capable of being. Look out world!

11 MONDAY ☿ *Moon Age Day 15 Moon Sign Taurus*

There could be some slight conflict today. It will probably be with colleagues if you are at work or maybe with a friend if you are not. Positive situations may come through family members and might also be evident if you take the trouble to rummage through the attic to find what someone thinks is a treasure.

12 TUESDAY ☿ *Moon Age Day 16 Moon Sign Taurus*

Your imagination could well be working overtime today and that's a mixed blessing. If you are planning for the future that's great, but there is always the possibility you will be inventing things to worry about. There are many situations that are beyond your own control and none of them are worth a moment of concern.

13 WEDNESDAY ☿ *Moon Age Day 17 Moon Sign Taurus*

There's just a slight tendency for you to dither today – maybe you've caught the habit from others around you? Where major decisions are concerned you are now more likely to weigh things in the balance and that could lead to some delays. Family parties are indicated, and if they are a possibility you will want to do some of the organising.

14 THURSDAY ☿ *Moon Age Day 18 Moon Sign Gemini*

Though there is still plenty going on, you would be well advised to stay away from major decision-making for today and tomorrow. In every other respect you will hardly notice the lunar low this month but you can get yourself in hot water if you try to move any goalposts or make pots of money.

15 FRIDAY ☿ *Moon Age Day 19   Moon Sign Gemini*

This should be another generally good day, despite the position of the Moon. You have what it takes to keep going, even when others are falling by the wayside. It is possible that by the end of the day you will be feeling somewhat lacking in sparkle, but that is your opinion and isn't one with which others would agree.

16 SATURDAY ☿ *Moon Age Day 20   Moon Sign Cancer*

There are favourable trends around for financial dealings of any sort though you will need to keep your eyes open for people who are not quite what they might seem. If you have to sign any contract be sure to look at these carefully and be on your guard against any sort of fraudster.

17 SUNDAY ☿ *Moon Age Day 21   Moon Sign Cancer*

There can be a great sense of both fulfilment and security around at the moment and you are likely to choose to stay close to home and family when you can. The attitudes of some of your colleagues might make work a less than wonderful experience but if you don't work at the weekend this could pass you by. If you are affected, keep your head down and work hard.

18 MONDAY ☿ *Moon Age Day 22   Moon Sign Leo*

A continuing trend that has a strong bearing on money matters might find you slightly better off than you expected now. People may willingly put themselves out for you and will be giving you plenty of advice, even when you haven't asked for it. Be sure of yourself before taking any sort of risk.

19 TUESDAY ☿ *Moon Age Day 23   Moon Sign Leo*

It seems that you are now very concerned with making outright progress, especially at work. If you are between jobs at the moment this ought to be a good time to keep your eyes and ears open. People want to do you favours, though once again it's rather unlikely that all of them will be particularly welcome.

20 WEDNESDAY ☿ *Moon Age Day 24   Moon Sign Leo*

Financial and business trends are going to be a slightly mixed bag today. There is a strong tendency for things to seem distinctly unsettled so you might be unable to feel totally comfortable in any given situation. Your confidence grows with the day but you are not going to feel like trying to move any mountains right now.

21 THURSDAY *Moon Age Day 25   Moon Sign Virgo*

Your quick thinking could save the day now. There are gains to be made in a number of different areas of your life but romance is probably going to be the best of all. If your partner has confidence in you, then it seems almost anything is possible. Allow some time today for having some fun.

22 FRIDAY *Moon Age Day 26   Moon Sign Virgo*

This is a good time for pleasant conversations in good company. Although you can't expect to get on well with everyone, there is the chance you could bury the hatchet with a certain person and your diplomatic skills should come in handy with friends. Where a new project is concerned, attitude is important.

23 SATURDAY *Moon Age Day 27   Moon Sign Libra*

Good ideas are now easy to come by and you won't go short of the sort of attention that allows you to preen yourself a little. Affection can come from the strangest of directions under present trends and there is no doubt about your ability to get most things right the first time round.

24 SUNDAY *Moon Age Day 28   Moon Sign Libra*

Today should be good for family life and you are likely to be on your best behaviour when dealing with those with whom you don't always agree. However, for better or worse you are likely to speak your mind – so if you are at work take care that this does not get you into a scrape. Tonight should be excellent for a romantic date.

25 MONDAY *Moon Age Day 29   Moon Sign Scorpio*

Though you should take care not to become sidetracked at the moment, you can't expect to be on the go all the time. Monday this week needs to be a time during which you can collect your thoughts. Trends in your chart strongly highlight the written word, so perhaps you will have your head in a good book.

26 TUESDAY *Moon Age Day 0   Moon Sign Scorpio*

As you throw your time and energies into your ambitions, in some ways a fresh start may be called for. This might not be too easy for you because certain planetary trends conspire to hold you back. Extra effort is necessary but with a good push you can get more or less where you want to be.

27 WEDNESDAY *Moon Age Day 1   Moon Sign Sagittarius*

Discussions will result in you feeling more satisfied with situations in a generally optimistic frame of mind. Your greatest gift right now lies in being able to make other people so happy. You have a very positive attitude to most aspects of life and can lift the spirits of those who have been sad of late.

28 THURSDAY *Moon Age Day 2   Moon Sign Sagittarius*

This would be an excellent period for telling someone how things really are. Although you might have been slightly shy of facing up to a particular person, today is an exception. Stand up for what you believe to be true and you may be surprised at how willingly others defer to your opinion.

29 FRIDAY *Moon Age Day 3   Moon Sign Capricorn*

Your capacity for getting ahead is still less than you would wish and a certain amount of frustration could be the result. Patience is called for, at a time when you don't seem to have much. Your creative powers are not diminished, however, and this would be an ideal time to do a little DIY.

30 SATURDAY   *Moon Age Day 4   Moon Sign Capricorn*

You should now take positive action to expand your financial horizons and trends suggest that you could make a gain as a result of someone else's mistake. Although you are looking closely at money, this isn't your sole motivation in life at the moment. Close, personal ties are also on the agenda and you are doing what you can to strengthen them.

December

2019

1 SUNDAY
Moon Age Day 5   Moon Sign Aquarius

Practical matters may be a little fraught today and this might be because you are trying to do too many things at the same time. Success is possible in a romantic sense, though even here you could find your partner or sweetheart proving to be slightly awkward. Stop and think things through carefully.

2 MONDAY
Moon Age Day 6   Moon Sign Aquarius

There is plain sailing in partnerships and a feeling that most things are going more or less the way you would wish. While you may need to plan for the medium-term, there are bound to be hiccups because of the Christmas period. Bear this in mind before you set anything in stone.

3 TUESDAY
Moon Age Day 7   Moon Sign Aquarius

Romance is powerfully accented today and your personal relationships seem to be running very smoothly now that the planets are lining up well for you. To others you appear charming and seem to know everything. As a result you are clearly being noticed and singled out for very special treatment.

4 WEDNESDAY
Moon Age Day 8   Moon Sign Pisces

Difficulties between yourself and your partner might have more to do with pressures from the outside world than any personal disagreements. It would be good to look at things from a distance and not to allow others to impinge on your deepest attachments. You need to relax today.

5 THURSDAY
Moon Age Day 9   Moon Sign Pisces

Things are likely to get off to a fairly slow start but as the day wears on you should notice a gradual quickening of pace. Be bold when it comes to speaking your mind because most people will be delighted to hear your point of view. Although you are likely to be a little lacking in confidence at the moment this situation won't last long.

6 FRIDAY
Moon Age Day 10   Moon Sign Aries

Get rid of situations that are not doing you any good at all – this should be easy to do under present trends. This might not be a bad time for clearing the decks for actions that are to come later and will probably be the last chance you have to do so before life really begins to get hectic.

7 SATURDAY
Moon Age Day 11   Moon Sign Aries

Everyday matters are likely to keep you busy this weekend but you should also find time to get together with friends, some of whom are proving to be highly entertaining at the moment. The weekend ought to give you the chance to stop and take stock but it's quite obvious that you are also up for a good time.

8 SUNDAY
Moon Age Day 12   Moon Sign Aries

Mental stimulation is the key for this Sunday. What you don't want is to be so bogged down with boring routines that you have no time to think. The Archer is very ingenious at the best of times but that ingenuity is going off the scale today. Others find you to be charismatic and very attractive.

9 MONDAY
Moon Age Day 13   Moon Sign Taurus

Social relationships continue to bring bigger and better times and you know how to turn heads. Contrary to the beliefs of some people you are successful in matters that haven't exactly been your forte before and you have a great commitment to anything you undertake. This should be an excellent day.

10 TUESDAY
Moon Age Day 14   Moon Sign Taurus

The emphasis at the moment is on a broad-minded outlook, which is not unusual for your zodiac sign. Routines can be very useful but at the same time you are now looking well ahead and the prospect of what lies before you in more than one way ought to be quite stimulating.

11 WEDNESDAY
Moon Age Day 15   Moon Sign Gemini

You could be rather too sensitive for your own good today and it might be sensible to take a laid-back view of life generally. The chances are that nobody is deliberately setting out to upset you even if that's the way it seems. In a personal sense you might be confronting a few demons at any time now.

12 THURSDAY
Moon Age Day 16   Moon Sign Gemini

You are likely to have less energy now and if this is the case you will have to coast through situations that usually see you soaring. At least you are getting the lunar low out of the way before the Christmas period gets started and you can rely on others to do some of the work at present. Plan now for events in the new year.

13 FRIDAY
Moon Age Day 17   Moon Sign Cancer

Things should now be going well at work, although there you may have some reservations and also may not be as efficient as would usually be the case. Realising that Christmas is now so close might not help because there is probably still a great deal to get done, in amongst a busy schedule.

14 SATURDAY
Moon Age Day 18   Moon Sign Cancer

There are many priorities to be dealt with just now and once again you could discover that time is of the essence. Pass some of these tasks to other people. Friends in particular should be happy to lend a hand and want to do whatever they can to lessen your burden in life.

15 SUNDAY
Moon Age Day 19   Moon Sign Cancer

You can successfully broaden the number of social contacts who are important to your life now and who will play an even bigger part later. Doing half a dozen different things at the same time should come as second nature to you and there is also the possibility of some financial gains that are basically down to luck.

16 MONDAY
Moon Age Day 20   Moon Sign Leo

Financially speaking, things now tend to look particularly bright. Of course any minor gains made at the moment are not likely to stay around long because the approach of Christmas is likely to see you spending fairly freely. However, you can still expect to wallow in life's little luxuries now if you get the chance.

17 TUESDAY
Moon Age Day 21   Moon Sign Leo

Versatility seems to be the chief key to success around now and you won't have any trouble at all keeping up with the general flow of life. Although you might come across one or two small stumbling blocks at work, in the main your progress is more than steady and at the same time social trends look good.

18 WEDNESDAY
Moon Age Day 22   Moon Sign Virgo

Whilst you should find yourself pretty much on target with regard to your general aims in life, there are possible little setbacks that are down to a quieter streak within your nature. Maybe you don't have quite the level of confidence to get things running your way practically or financially? The answer is easy – enlist some support.

19 THURSDAY
Moon Age Day 23   Moon Sign Virgo

Some of the pressures coming in from the outside world should lessen at this time and it is now possible to commit yourself almost fully to what lies ahead in terms of the celebrations. Archers generally love Christmas, even if a few of you try to pretend that this is not the case. Socialise whenever possible.

20 FRIDAY
Moon Age Day 24   Moon Sign Libra

Practical matters run smoothly enough and you should be contributing a very joyful attitude to whatever is going on around you at this time. Today would be favourable for organising and for getting an overview of where you are at the moment. There ought to be time for extreme activity but also for some relaxation.

21 SATURDAY
Moon Age Day 25   Moon Sign Libra

You could do with keeping a fairly low profile today. This isn't because you are putting a dampener on things for others but merely because you might be feeling a little below par. Routines probably work best for you, and there is happiness to be found in your home environment. By the evening you should be feeling on better form.

22 SUNDAY
Moon Age Day 26   Moon Sign Scorpio

Domestic issues continue to be quite fulfilling and new social influences may help lighten the load if you feel that certain jobs are getting you down a little. With the big celebrations now in view it is just possible that you are lacking a little sparkle. Compensate for this with your organisational skills.

23 MONDAY
Moon Age Day 27   Moon Sign Scorpio

Close emotional involvements appeal to you and the nostalgic nature of the Christmas period has hold of you. Anything to do with carol singers or chestnuts roasting on an open fire will appeal as you are inclined to turn towards the more old-fashioned way of celebrating the time of year.

24 TUESDAY
Moon Age Day 28   Moon Sign Sagittarius

This Christmas Eve looks very good for Sagittarius, with lots and energy and the lunar high helping you to get what you want from life. You may be faced with all sorts of possibilities, all of which you deal with efficiently and with style. Plans for tomorrow are probably in full swing already and the social scene begins right now.

25 WEDNESDAY *Moon Age Day 29   Moon Sign Sagittarius*

You find the right kind of opportunities necessary to get ahead on Christmas Day. Even little things can be seized upon, and mentally set aside to give you a professional edge in the new year. While you may also benefit from a little good luck, and might therefore be in the mood to take a gamble, a little care would still be advisable.

26 THURSDAY *Moon Age Day 0   Moon Sign Capricorn*

Boxing Day promises much because you should be feeling quite happy and confident as you continue the festivities. Being naturally caring and giving, you get a great deal of your own joy from the way others have a good time. Share yourself between your partner, your family and friends.

27 FRIDAY *Moon Age Day 1   Moon Sign Capricorn*

It may be necessary to make some small changes to an aspect of your personal life and you won't be short of advice on this score. Friends are only too willing to share their wisdom with you though it might be in doubt how much they actually know. In the end it would definitely be best to suit yourself.

28 SATURDAY *Moon Age Day 2   Moon Sign Capricorn*

Contacts made at this time are not only interesting but are also likely to be extremely useful in the fullness of time. You will no doubt enjoy taking a centre-stage position because the Archer is one of the most gregarious of all the zodiac signs. You can do much to improve the general attitude of family members.

29 SUNDAY *Moon Age Day 3   Moon Sign Aquarius*

Some fairly down-to-earth talks with certain people could bring in useful information at this time and sees you getting ahead of the field in some way. Personalities abound and you seem to have that vital spark that others are looking for. If this gets you a great deal of attention don't be unduly surprised.

30 MONDAY
Moon Age Day 4   Moon Sign Aquarius

Don't believe everything you hear today because at least a proportion of it won't be true. You have everything necessary to make a good impression and for some of you a brand new relationship is already looking good. Trends indicate a minor illness of some sort, so don't take any chances with leftover food.

31 TUESDAY
Moon Age Day 5   Moon Sign Pisces

Matters connected with the past are beneficially highlighted under the planetary trends for this New Year's Eve. A chance to review an old issue should not be missed, whilst at the same time you are very committed to what lies ahead. New friendships could be formed while you enjoy the party atmosphere.

RISING SIGNS FOR SAGITTARIUS

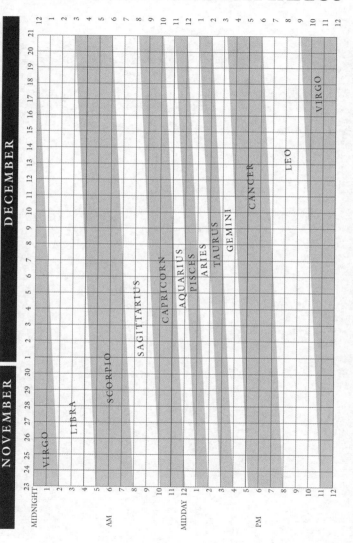

THE ZODIAC, PLANETS AND CORRESPONDENCES

The Earth revolves around the Sun once every calendar year, so when viewed from Earth the Sun appears in a different part of the sky as the year progresses. In astrology, these parts of the sky are divided into the signs of the zodiac and this means that the signs are organised in a circle. The circle begins with Aries and ends with Pisces.

Taking the zodiac sign as a starting point, astrologers then work with all the positions of planets, stars and many other factors to calculate horoscopes and birth charts and tell us what the stars have in store for us.

The table below shows the planets and Elements for each of the signs of the zodiac. Each sign belongs to one of the four Elements: Fire, Air, Earth or Water. Fire signs are creative and enthusiastic; Air signs are mentally active and thoughtful; Earth signs are constructive and practical; Water signs are emotional and have strong feelings.

It also shows the metals and gemstones associated with, or corresponding with, each sign. The correspondence is made when a metal or stone possesses properties that are held in common with a particular sign of the zodiac.

Finally, the table shows the opposite of each star sign – this is the opposite sign in the astrological circle.

Placed	Sign	Symbol	Element	Planet	Metal	Stone	Opposite
1	Aries	Ram	Fire	Mars	Iron	Bloodstone	Libra
2	Taurus	Bull	Earth	Venus	Copper	Sapphire	Scorpio
3	Gemini	Twins	Air	Mercury	Mercury	Tiger's Eye	Sagittarius
4	Cancer	Crab	Water	Moon	Silver	Pearl	Capricorn
5	Leo	Lion	Fire	Sun	Gold	Ruby	Aquarius
6	Virgo	Maiden	Earth	Mercury	Mercury	Sardonyx	Pisces
7	Libra	Scales	Air	Venus	Copper	Sapphire	Aries
8	Scorpio	Scorpion	Water	Pluto	Plutonium	Jasper	Taurus
9	Sagittarius	Archer	Fire	Jupiter	Tin	Topaz	Gemini
10	Capricorn	Goat	Earth	Saturn	Lead	Black Onyx	Cancer
11	Aquarius	Waterbearer	Air	Uranus	Uranium	Amethyst	Leo
12	Pisces	Fishes	Water	Neptune	Tin	Moonstone	Virgo